Poems

Wherein It Is Attempted To Describe Certain Views Of Nature And
Of Rustic Manners; And Also, To Point Out, In Some Instances,
The Different Influence Which The Same Circumstances Produce
On Different Characters

Joanna Baillie

Contents

POEMS

BY

Joanna Baillie

POEMS;

WHEREIN IT IS ATTEMPTED TO DESCRIBE
CERTAIN VIEWS OF NATURE AND OF
RUSTIC MANNERS; AND ALSO,

TO POINT OUT, IN SOME INSTANCES, THE DIFFERENT INFLUENCE
WHICH THE SAME
CIRCUMSTANCES PRODUCE ON DIFFERENT CHARACTERS.

A WINTER DAY.

The cock, warm roosting 'midst his feather'd dames,
Now lifts his beak and snuffs the morning air,
Stretches his neck and claps his heavy wings,
Gives three hoarse crows, and glad his talk is done;
Low, chuckling, turns himself upon the roost,
Then nestles down again amongst his mates.
The lab'ring hind, who on his bed of straw,
Beneath his home-made coverings, coarse, but warm,
Lock'd in the kindly arms of her who spun them,
Dreams of the gain that next year's crop should bring;
Or at some fair disposing of his wool,
Or by some lucky and unlook'd-for bargain.
Fills his skin purse with heaps of tempting gold,

Now wakes from sleep at the unwelcome call,
And finds himself but just the same poor man
As when he went to rest.--
He hears the blast against his window beat,
And wishes to himself he were a lord,
That he might lie a-bed.--
He rubs his eyes, and stretches out his arms;
Heigh ho! heigh ho! he drawls with gaping mouth,
Then most unwillingly creeps out of bed,
And without looking-glass puts on his clothes.
With rueful face he blows the smother'd fire,
And lights his candle at the red'ning coal;
First sees that all be right amongst his cattle,
Then hies him to the barn with heavy tread,
Printing his footsteps on the new fall'n snow.
From out the heap of corn he pulls his sheaves,
Dislodging the poor red-breast from his shelter,
Where all the live-long night he slept secure;
But now afrighted, with uncertain flight
He flutters round the walls, to seek some hole,
At which he may escape out to the frost.
And now the flail, high whirling o'er his head,
Descends with force upon the jumping sheave,
Whilst every rugged wall, and neighboring cot
Re-echoes back the noise of his strokes.

   The fam'ly cares call next upon the wife
To quit her mean but comfortable bed.
And first she stirs the fire, and blows the flame,
Then from her heap of sticks, for winter stor'd,
An armful brings; loud crackling as they burn,
Thick fly the red sparks upward to the roof,
While slowly mounts the smoke in wreathy clouds.

On goes the seething pot with morning cheer,
For which some little wishful hearts await,
Who, peeping from the bed-clothes, spy, well pleas'd,
The cheery light that blazes on the wall,
And bawl for leave to rise.----
Their busy mother knows not where to turn,
Her morning work comes now so thick upon her.
One she must help to tye his little coat,
Unpin his cap, and seck another's shoe.
When all is o'er, out to the door they run,
With new comb'd sleeky hair, and glist'ning cheeks,
Each with some little project in his head.
One on the ice must try his new sol'd shoes:
To view his well-set trap another hies,
In hopes to find some poor unwary bird
(No worthless prize) entangled in his snare;
Whilst one, less active, with round rosy face,
Spreads out his purple fingers to the fire,
And peeps, most wishfully, into the pot.

  But let us leave the warm and cheerful house,
To view the bleak and dreary scene without,
And mark the dawning of a winter day.
For now the morning vapour, red and grumly,
Rests heavy on the hills; and o'er the heav'ns
Wide spreading forth in lighter gradual fliades,
Just faintly colours the pale muddy sky.
Then slowly from behind the southern hills,
Inlarg'd and ruddy looks the rising sun,
Shooting his beams askance the hoary waste,
Which gild the brow of ev'ry swelling height,
And deepen every valley with a shade.
The crusted window of each scatter'd cot,

The icicles that fringe the thatched roof,
The new swept slide upon the frozen pool,
All lightly glance, new kindled with his rays;
And e'en the rugged face of scowling Winter
Looks somewhat gay. But for a little while
He lifts his glory o'er the bright'ning earth,
Then hides his head behind a misty cloud,

  The birds now quit their holes and lurking sheds,
Most mute and melancholy, where thro' night
All nestling close to keep each other warm,
In downy sleep they had forgot their hardships;
But not to chant and carol in the air,
Or lightly swing upon some waving bough,
And merrily return each other's notes;
No; silently they hop from bush to bush,
Yet find no seeds to stop their craving want,
Then bend their flight to the low smoking cot,
Chirp on the roof, or at the window peck,
To tell their wants to those who lodge within.
The poor lank hare flies homeward to his den,
But little burthen'd with his nightly meal
Of wither'd greens grubb'd from the farmer's garden;
A poor and scanty portion snatch'd in fear;
And fearful creatures, forc'd abroad by want,
Are now to ev'ry enemy a prey.

  The husbandman lays bye his heavy flail,
And to the house returns, where on him wait
His smoking breakfast and impatient children;
Who, spoon in hand, and longing to begin,
Towards the door cast many a weary look
To see their dad come in.----

Then round they sit, a chearful company,
All eagerly begin, and with heap'd spoons
Besmear from ear to ear their rosy cheeks.
The faithful dog stands by his matter's side
Wagging his tail, and looking in his face;
While humble puss pays court to all around,
And purs and rubs them with her furry sides;
Nor goes this little flattery unrewarded.
But the laborious sit not long at table;
The grateful father lifts his eyes to heav'n
To bless his God, whose ever bounteous hand
Him and his little ones doth daily feed;
Then rises satisfied to work again.

  The chearful rousing noise of industry
Is heard, with varied sounds, thro' all the village.
The humming wheel, the thrifty housewife's tongue,
Who scolds to keep her maidens at their work,
Rough grating cards, and voice of squaling children
Issue from every house.----
But, hark!--the sportsman from the neighb'ring hedge
His thunder sends!--loud bark each village cur;
Up from her wheel each curious maiden starts,
And hastens to the door, whilst matrons chide,
Yet run to look themselves, in spite of thrift,
And all the little town is in a stir.

  Strutting before, the cock leads forth his train,
And, chuckling near the barn among the straw,
Reminds the farmer of his morning's service;
His grateful master throws a lib'ral handful;
They flock about it, whilst the hungry sparrows
Perch'd on the roof, look down with envious eye,

Then, aiming well, amidst the feeders light,
And seize upon the feast with greedy bill,
Till angry partlets peck them off the field.
But at a distance, on the leafless tree,
All woe be gone, the lonely blackbird sits;
The cold north wind ruffles his glossy feathers;
Full oft' he looks, but dare not make approach;
Then turns his yellow bill to peck his side,
And claps his wings close to his sharpen'd breast.
The wand'ring fowler, from behind the hedge,
Fastens his eye upon him, points his gun,
And firing wantonly as at a mark,
E'en lays him low in that same cheerful spot
Which oft' hath ccho'd with his ev'ning's song.

   The day now at its height, the pent-up kine
Are driven from their flails to take the air.
How stupidly they stare! and feel how strange!
They open wide their smoking mouths to low,
But scarcely can their feeble sound be heard;
Then turn and lick themselves, and step by step
Move dull and heavy to their flails again.
In scatter'd groups the little idle boys
With purple fingers, moulding in the snow
Their icy ammunition, pant for war;
And, drawing up in opposite array,
Send forth a mighty fliower of well aim'd balls,
Whilst little hero's try their growing flrength,
And burn to beat the en'my off the field.
Or on the well worn ice in eager throngs,
Aiming their race, shoot rapidly along,
Trip up each other's heels, and on the surface
With knotted shoes, draw many a chalky line.

Untir'd of play, they never cease their sport
Till the faint sun has almost run his course,
And threat'ning clouds, slow rising from the north,
Spread grumly darkness o'er the face of heav'n;
Then, by degrees, they scatter to their homes,
With many a broken head and bloody nose,
To claim their mothers' pity, who, most skilful,
Cures all their troubles with a bit of bread.

   The night comes on a pace----
Chill blows the blast, and drives the snow in wreaths.
Now ev'ry creature looks around for shelter,
And, whether man or beast, all move alike
Towards their several homes; and happy they
Who have a house to screen them from the cold!
Lo, o'er the frost a rev'rend form advances!
His hair white as the snow on which he treads,
His forehead mark'd with many a care-worn furrow,
Whose feeble body, bending o'er a staff,
Still shew that once it was the seat of strength,
Tho' now it shakes like some old ruin'd tow'r,
Cloth'd indeed, but not disgrac'd with rags,
He still maintains that decent dignity
Which well becomes those who have serv'd their country.
With tott'ring steps he to the cottage moves:
The wife within, who hears his hollow cough,
And patt'ring of iris stick upon the threshold,
Sends out her little boy to see who's there.
The child looks up to view the stranger's face,
And seeing it enlighten'd with a smile,
Holds out his little hand to lead him in.
Rous'd from her work, the mother turns her head,
And sees them, not ill-pleas'd.----

The stranger whines not with a piteous tale,
But only asks a little, to relieve
A poor old soldier's wants.----
The gentle matron brings the ready chair,
And bids him sit, to rest his wearied limbs,
And warm himself before her blazing fire.
The children, full of curiosity,
Flock round, and with their fingers in their mouths,
Stand staring at him; whilst the stranger, pleas'd,
Takes up the youngest boy upon his knee.
Proud of its seat, it wags its little feet,
And prates, and laughs, and plays with his white locks.
But soon the soldier's face lays off its smiles;
His thoughtful mind is turn'd on other days,
When his own boys were wont to play around him,
Who now lie distant from their native land
In honourable, but untimely graves.
He feels how helpless and forlorn he is,
And bitter tears gush from his dim-worn eyes.
His toilsome daily labour at an end,
In comes the wearied master of the house,
And marks with satisfaction his old guest,
With all his children round.--
His honest heart is fill'd with manly kindness;
He bids him stay, and share their homely meal,
And take with them his quarters for the night.
The weary wanderer thankfully accepts,
And, seated with the cheerful family,
Around the plain but hospitable board,
Forgets the many hardships he has pass'd.

  When all are satisfied, about the fire
They draw their seats, and form a cheerful ring.

The thrifty housewife turns her spinning wheel;
The husband, useful even in his rest,
A little basket weaves of willow twigs,
To bear her eggs to town on market days;
And work but serves t'enliven conversation.
Some idle neighbours now come straggling in,
Draw round their chairs, and widen out the circle.
Without a glass the tale and jest go round;
And every one, in his own native way,
Does what he can to cheer the merry group.
Each tells some little story of himself,
That constant subject upon which mankind,
Whether in court or country, love to dwell.
How at a fair he sav'd a simple clown
From being tricked in buying of a cow;
Or laid a bet upon his horse's head
Against his neighbour's, bought for twice his price,
Which fail'd not to repay his better skill:
Or on a harvest day, bound in an hour
More sheaves of corn than any of his fellows,
Tho' ne'er so keen, could do in twice the time.
But chief the landlord, at his own fire-side,
Doth claim the right of being listen'd to;
Nor dares a little bawling tongue be heard,
Tho' but in play, to break upon his story.
The children sit and listen with the rest;
And should the youngest raise its little voice,
The careful mother, ever on the watch,
And always pleas'd with what her husband says,
Gives it a gentle tap upon the fingers,
Or stops its ill tim'd prattle with a kiss.
The soldier next, but not unask'd, begins,
And tells in better speech what he has seen;

Making his simple audience to shrink
With tales of war and blood. They gaze upon him,
And almost weep to see the man so poor,
So bent and feeble, helpless and forlorn,
That oft' has stood undaunted in the battle
Whilst thund'ring cannons shook the quaking earth,
And showering bullets hiss'd around his head.
With little care they pass away the night,
Till time draws on when they should go to bed;
Then all break up, and each retires to rest
With peaceful mind, nor torn with vexing cares,
Nor dancing with the unequal beat of pleasure.

  But long accustom'd to observe the weather,
The labourer cannot lay him down in peace
Till he has look'd to mark what bodes the night,
He turns the heavy door, thrusts out his head,
Sees wreathes of snow heap'd up on ev'ry side,
And black and grimily all above his head,
Save when a red gleam shoots along the waste
To make the gloomy night more terrible
Loud blows the northern blast----
He hears it hollow grumbling from afar,
Then, gath'ring strength, roll on with doubl'd might,
And break in dreadful bellowings o'er his head;
Like pithless saplings bend the vexed trees,
And their wide branches crack. He shuts the door,
And, thankful for the roof that covers him,
Hies him to bed.

A SUMMER DAY.

The dark-blue clouds of night in dusky lines,
Drawn wide and streaky o'er the purer sky,
Wear faint the morning purple on their skirts.
The stars that full and bright shone in the west,
But dimly twinkle to the stedfast eye;
And seen, and vanishing, and seen again,
Like dying tapers smoth'ring in their sockets,
Appear at last shut from the face of heav'n;
Whilst every lesser flame which shone by night,
The flashy meteor from the op'ning cloud,
That shoots full oft' across the dusky sky;
Or wand'ring fire which looks across the marsh,
Beaming like candle in a lonely cot,
To cheer the hopes of the benighted trav'ller,
Till swifter than the very change of thought,
It shifts from place to place, escapes his glance,
And makes him wond'ring rub his doubtful eyes;
Or humble glow-worm, or the silver moth,
Which cast a feeble glimm'ring o'er the green,
All die away.----
For now the sun, slow moving in his grandeur,
Above the eastern mountains lifts his head.
The webs of dew spread o'er the hoary lawn,
The smooth clear bosom of the settled pool,
The polish'd ploughshare on the distant field,
Catch fire from him, and dart their new got beams
Upon die dazzled eye.

  The new-wak'd birds upon the branches hop,
Peck their loft down, and bristle out their feathers;

Then stretch their throats and tune their morning song;
Whilst stately crows, high swinging o'er their heads.
Upon the topmost boughs, in lordly pride,
Mix their hoarse croaking with the linnet's note;
Till gather'd closer in a sable band,
They take their flight to leek their daily food.
The village labourer, with careful mind,
As soon as doth the morning light appear,
Opens his eyes with the first darting ray
That pierces thro' the window of his cot,
And quits his easy bed; then o'er the field,
With lengthen'd swinging strides, betakes his way,
Bearing his spade and hoe across his moulder,
Seen from afar clear glancing in the sun,
And with good will begins his daily work.
The sturdy sun-burnt boy drives forth the cattle,
And vain of power, bawls to the lagging kine,
Who fain would stay to crop the tender shoots
Of the green tempting hedges as they pass;
Or beats the glist'ning bushes with his club,
To please his fancy with a shower of dew,
And frighten the poor birds who lurk within.
At ev'ry open door, thro' all the village,
Half naked children, half awake, are seen
Scratching their heads, and blinking to the light;
Till roused by degrees, they run about,
Or rolling in the sun, amongst the sand
Build many a little house, with heedful art.
The housewife tends within, her morning care;
And stooping 'midst her tubs of curdled milk,
With busy patience, draws the clear green whey
From the press'd sides of the pure snowy curd;
Whilst her brown dimpled maid, with tuck'd-up sleeve,

And swelling arm, assists her in her toil.
Pots smoke, pails rattle, and the warm confusion
Still thickens on them, till within its mould,
With careful hands, they press the well-wrought curd.

　So goes the morning, till the pow'rful sun
High in the heav'ns sends forth his strengthen'd beams,
And all the freshness of the morn is fled.
The sweating trav'ller throws his burden down,
And leans his weary shoulder 'gainst a tree.
The idle horse upon the grassy field
Rolls on his back, nor heeds the tempting clover.
The swain leaves off his labour, and returns
Slow to his house with heavy sober steps,
Where on the board his ready breakfast plac'd,
Invites the eye, and his right cheerful wife
Doth kindly serve him with unfeign'd good will.
No sparkling dew-drops hang upon the grass;
Forth steps the mower with his glitt'ring scythe,
In snowy shirt, and doublet all unbrac'd,
White moves he o'er the ridge, with sideling bend,
And lays the waving grass in many a heap.
In ev'ry field, in ev'ry swampy mead,
The cheerful voice of industry is heard;
The hay-cock rises, and the frequent rake
Sweeps on the yellow hay, in heavy wreaths,
Leaving the smooth green meadow bare behind.
The old and young, the weak and strong are there,
And, as they can, help on the cheerful work.
The father jeers his awkward half-grown lad,
Who trails his tawdry armful o'er the field,
Nor does he fear the jeering to repay.
The village oracle, and simple maid,

Jest in their turns, and raise the ready laugh;
For there authority, hard favour'd, frowns not;
All are companions in the gen'ral glee,
And cheerful complaisance still thro' their roughness,
With placid look enlightens ev'ry face.
Some more advanced raise the tow'ring rick,
Whilst on its top doth stand the parish toast
In loose attire, and swelling ruddy cheek;
With taunts and harmless mock'ry she receives
The toss'd-up heaps from the brown gaping youth,
Who flaring at her, takes his aim awry,
Whilst half the load comes tumbling on himself.
Loud is her laugh, her voice is heard afar;
Each mower, busied in the distant field,
The carter, trudging on his distant way,
The shrill found know, cad up their hats in air,
And roar across the fields to catch her notice:
She waves her arm, and shakes her head at them,
And then renews her work with double spirit.
Thus do they jest, and laugh away their toil,
Till the bright sun, full in his middle course,
Shoots down his fiercest beams, which none may brave.
The stoutest arm hangs listless by its side,
And the broad shoulder'd youth begins to fail.
But to the weary, lo! there comes relief!
A troop of welcome children, o'er the lawn,
With slow and wary steps, their burthens bring.
Some bear upon their heads large baskets, heap'd
With piles of barley bread, and gusty cheese,
And some full pots of milk and cooling whey.
Beneath the branches of a spreading tree,
Or by the shad'wy side of the tall rick,
They spread their homely fare, and seated round,

Taste all the pleasure that a feast can give.

A drowzy indolence now hangs on all,
And ev'ry creature seeks some place of rest,
Screen'd from the violence of the oppressive heat.
No scatter'd flocks are seen upon the lawn,
Nor chirping birds among the bushes heard.
Within the narrow shadow of the cot
The sleepy dog lies stretched on his side,
Nor heeds the heavy-footed passenger;
At noise of feet but half his eye-lid lifts,
Then gives a feeble growl, and sleeps again:
Whilst puss, less nice, e'en in the scorching window,
On t'other side, sits winking to the sun.
No sound is heard but humming of the bee,
For she alone retires not from her labour,
Nor leaves a meadow flower unsought for gain.

Heavy and slow so pass the mid-day hours,
Till gently bending on the ridge's top,
The heavy seeded grass begins to wave,
And the high branches of the slender poplar
Shiver aloft in air their rustling leaves.
Cool breaths the rising breeze, and with it wakes
The worn out spirit from its state of stupor.
The lazy boy springs from his mossy bed,
To chace the gaudy tempting butterfly,
Who spreading on the grass its mealy wings,
Oft lights within his reach, e'en at his seer,
Yet still eludes his grasp, and o'er his head
Light hov'ring round, or mounted high in air
Temps his young eye, and wearies out his limbs.
The drouzy dog, who feels the kindly breeze

That passing o'er him, lifts his shaggy ear,
Begins to stretch him, on his legs half-rais'd,
Till fully wak'd, with bristling cock'd-up tail,
He makes the village echo to his bark.

  But let us not forget the busy maid
Who, by the side of the clear pebly stream,
Spreads out her snowy linens to the sun,
And sheds with lib'ral hand the chrystal show'r
O'er many a fav'rite piece of fair attire,
Revolving in her mind her gay appearance
In all this dress, at some approaching fair.
The dimpling half-check'd smile, and mutt'ring lip
Betray the secret workings of her fancy,
And flattering thoughts of the complacent mind.
There little vagrant bands of truant boys
Amongst the bushes try their harmless tricks;
Whilst some a sporting in the shallow stream
Toss up the lashing water round their heads,
Or strive with wily art to catch the trout,
Or 'twixt their fingers grasp the slipp'ry eel.
The shepherd-boy sits singing on the bank,
To pass away the weary lonely hours,
Weaving with art his little crown of rushes,
A guiltless easy crown that brings no care,
Which having made he places on his head,
And leaps and skips about, and bawls full loud
To some companion, lonely as himself,
Far in the distant field; or else delighted
To hear the echo'd sound of his own voice
Returning answer from the neighboring rock,
Holds no unpleasing converse with himself.

Now weary labourers perceive, well-pleas'd,
The shadows lengthen, and th' oppressive day
With all its toil fast wearing to an end.
The sun, far in the west, with side-long beam
Plays on the yellow head of the round hay-cock,
And fields are checker'd with fantastic shapes
Or tree, or shrub, or gate, or rugged stone,
All lengthen'd out, in antic disproportion,
Upon the darken'd grass.----
They finish out their long and toilsome talk.
Then, gathering up their rakes and scatter'd coats,
With the less cumb'rous fragments of their feast,
Return right gladly to their peaceful homes.

The village, lone and silent thro' the day,
Receiving from the fields its merry bands,
Sends forth its ev'ning sound, confus'd but cheerful;
Whilst dogs and children, eager housewives' tongues,
And true love ditties, in no plaintive strain,
By shrill voic'd maid, at open window sung;
The lowing of the home-returning kine,
The herd's low droning trump, and tinkling bell
Tied to the collar of his fav'rite sheep,
Make no contemptible variety
To ears not over nice.----
With careless lounging gait, the saunt'ring youth
Upon his sweetheart's open window leans,
And as she turns about her buzzing wheel
Diverts her with his jokes and harmless taunts.
Close by the cottage door, with placid mien,
The old man sits upon his seat of turf,
His staff with crooked head laid by his side,
Which oft the younger race in wanton sport,

Gambolling round him, slyly steal away,
And straddling o'er it, shew their horsemanship
By raising round the clouds of summer sand,
While still he smiles, yet chides them for the trick.
His silver locks upon his shoulders spread,
And not ungraceful is his stoop of age.
No stranger passes him without regard;
And ev'ry neighbour stops to wish him well,
And ask him his opinion of the weather.
They fret not at the length of his discourse,
But listen with respect to his remarks
Upon the various seasons he remembers;
For well he knows the many divers signs
Which do fortell high winds, or rain, or drought,
Or ought that may affect the rising crop.
The silken clad, who courtly breeding boast,
Their own discourse still sweetest to their ears,
May grumble at the old man's lengthened story,
But here it is not so.----

  From ev'ry chimney mounts the curling smoke,
Muddy and gray, of the new ev'ning fire;
On ev'ry window smokes the fam'ly supper,
Set out to cool by the attentive housewife,
While cheerful groups at every door conven'd
Bawl cross the narrow lane the parish news,
And oft the bursting laugh disturbs the air.
But see who comes to set them all agag!
The weary-footed pedlar with his pack.
How stiff he bends beneath his bulky load!
Cover'd with dust, slip-shod, and out at elbows;
His greasy hat sits backward on his head;
His thin straight hair divided on his brow

Hangs lank on either side his glist'ning cheeks,
And woe-begone, yet vacant is his face.
His box he opens and displays his ware.
Full many a varied row of precious stones
Cast forth their dazzling lustre to the light.
To the desiring maiden's wishful eye
The ruby necklace shews its tempting blaze:
The china buttons, stamp'd with love device,
Attract the notice of the gaping youth;
Whilst streaming garters, fasten'd to a pole,
Aloft in air their gaudy stripes display,
And from afar the distant stragglers lure.
The children leave their play and round him flock;
E'en sober aged grand-dame quits her seat,
Where by the door she twines her lengthen'd threads,
Her spindle stops, and lays her distaff by,
Then joins with step sedate the curious throng.
She praises much the fashions of her youth,
And scorns each gaudy nonsense of the day;
Yet not ill-pleas'd the glossy ribband views,
Uproll'd, and changing hues with ev'ry fold,
New measur'd out to deck her daughter's head.

  Now red, but languid, the last weakly beams
Of the departing sun, across the lawn
Deep gild the top of the long sweepy ridge,
And shed a scatter'd brightness, bright but cheerless,
Between the op'nings of the rifted hills;
Which like the farewell looks of some dear friend,
That speaks him kind, yet sadden as they smile,
But only serve to deepen the low vale,
And make the shadows of the night more gloomy.
The varied noises of the cheerful village

By slow degrees now faintly die away,
And more distinct each feeble sound is heard
That gently steals ad own the river's bed,
Or thro' the wood comes with the ruffling breeze.
The white mist rises from the swampy glens,
And from the dappled flatting of the heav'ns
Looks out the ev'ning star.----
The lover skulking in the neighb'ring copse,
(Whose half-seen form shewn thro' the thicken'd air,
Large and majestic, makes the tray'ller start,
And spreads the story of the haunted grove,)
Curses the owl, whose loud ill-omen'd scream,
With ceaseless spite, robes from his watchful ear
The well known footsteps of his darling maid;
And fretful, chaces from his face the night-fly,
Who buzzing round his head doth often skim,
With flutt'ring wing, across his glowing cheek:
For all but him in deep and balmy sleep
Forget the toils of the oppressive day;
Shut is the door of ev'ry scatter'd cot,
And silence dwells within.

NIGHT SCENES OF OTHER TIMES.

A POEM, IN THREE PARTS.

PART I.

"The wild winds bellow o'er my head,
  And spent eve's fading light;

Where shall I find some friendly shed
  To screen me from the night?

"Ah! round me lies a desert vast,
  No habitation near;
And dark and pathless is the waste,
  And fills the mind with fear

"Thou distant tree, whose lonely top
  Has bent to many a storm,
No more canst thou deceive my hope,
  And take my lover's form;

"For o'er thy head the dark cloud rolls,
  Black as thy blasted pride.
How deep the angry tempest growls
  Along the mountain's side!

"Securely rests the mountain deer
  Within his hollow den,
His slumber undisturb'd by fear,
  Far from the haunts of men.

"Beneath the fern the moorcock sleeps,
  And twisted adders lie;
Back to his rock the night-bird creeps,
  Nor gives his wonted cry.

"For angry spirits of the night
  Ride in the troubled air,
And to their dens, in wild affright,
  The beasts of prey repair.

"But oh! my love! where do'st thou rest?
  What shelter covers thee?
O, may this cold and wint'ry blast
  But only beat on me!

"Some friendly dwelling may'st thou find,
  Where, undisturb'd with care,
Thou shalt not feel the chilly wind
  That ruffles Marg'ret's hair.

"Ah, no! for thou did'st give thy word
  To meet me on the way;
Nor friendly roof, nor coastly board
  Will tempt a lover's stay.

"O, raise thy voice, if thou art near!
  Its weakest sound were bliss:
What other sound my heart can cheer
  In such a gloom as this?

"But from the hills with stunning sound
  The dashing torrents fall;
Loud is the raging tempest round,
  And mocks a lover's call.

"Ha! see across the dreary waste
  A gentle form appears!
It is my love, my cares are past,
  How vain were all my fears?"

The form approach'd, but sad and slow,
  Nor with a lover's tread;
And from his cheek the youthful glow,

And greeting smile was fled.

Dim sadness hung upon his brow;
  Fix'd was his beamless eye:
His face was like the moon-light bow
  Upon a win'try sky.

And fix'd and ghastly to the sight,
  His strengthen'd features rose;
And bended was his graceful height,
  And bloody were his clothes.

"O Marg'ret, calm thy troubled breast!
  Thy sorrow now is vain:
Thy Edward from his peaceful rest
  Shall ne'er return again.

"A treach'rous friend has brought me low,
  And fix'd my early doom;
And laid my corpse, with feigned woe,
  Beneath a vaulted tomb

"To take thee to my home I sware,
  And here we were to meet:
Wilt thou a narrow coffin share,
  And part my winding-sheet?

"But late the lord of many lands,
  And now a grave is all:
My blood is warm upon his hands
  Who revels in my hall.

"Yet think thy father's hoary hair

Is water'd with his tears;
He has but thee to sooth his care,
  And prop his load of years.

"Remember Edward when he's gone,
  He only liv'd for thee;
And when thou'rt pensive, and alone,
  O Marg'ret call on me!

"Yet deep beneath the mould'ring clod
  I rest my wounded head:
And terrible that call, and loud,
  Which shall awake the dead."

"No, Edward, I will follow thee,
  And share thy hapless doom:
Companions shall our spirits be,
  Tho' distant is thy tomb.

"O! never to my father's tower
  Will I return again!
A bleeding heart has little power
  To ease another's pain.

"Upon the wing my spirit flies,
  I feel my course is run;
Nor shall these dim and weary eyes
  Behold to-morrow's sun."

Like early dew, or hoary frost,
  Spent with the beaming day,
So shrunk the pale and wat'ry ghost,
  And dimly wore away.

No longer Marg'ret felt the storm,
  She bow'd her lovely head;
And with her lover's fleeting form,
  Her gentle spirit fled.

PART II.

Loud roars the wind that shakes this wall;
  It is no common blast:
Deep hollow sounds pass thro' my hall,
  O would the night were past!

"Methinks the daemons of the air
  Upon the turrets growl;
While down the empty winding stair
  Their deep'ning murmurs roll.

"The glimm'ring fire cheers not the gloom:
  How blue its weakly ray!
And like a taper in a tomb,
  But spreads the more dismay.

"Athwart its melancholy light
  The lengthen'd shadow falls:
My grandsires, to my troubled sight,
  Low'r on me from these walls.

"Methinks yon angry warrior's head
  Doth in its casement frown,
And darts a look, as if it said,
  Where hast thou laid my son?

"But will these fancies never cease?
  O, would the night were run!
My troubled soul can find no peace,
  But with the morning sun.

"Vain hope! the guilty never rest;
  Dismay is always near:
There is a midnight in the breast
  No morn shall ever cheer.

"The weary hind is now at rest,
  Tho' lowly is his head,
How sweetly lies the guiltless breast,
  Upon the hardest bed!

"The beggar, in his wretched haunt,
  May now a monarch be;
Forget his woe, forget his want,
  For all can sleep but me.

"I've dar'd whate'er the boldest can,
  Then why this childish dread;
I never fear'd a living man,
  And shall I fear the dead!

"No, whistling storms may shake my tower,
  And passing spirits scream:
Their shadowy arms are void of power,
  And but a gloomy dream.

"But, lo! a form advancing slow
  Across my dusky hall!

Art thou a friend? art thou a foe?
  O, answer to my call!"

Still nearer to the glimm'ring light
  The tow'ring figure strode,
Till full, and horrid to the sight,
  The murther'd Edward stood.

His hand a broken dagger sway'd,
  Like Time's dark threat'ning dart;
And pointed to the rugged blade
  That quiver'd in his heart.

The blood still trickled from his head,
  And clotted was his hair,
That on his manly shoulders spread;
  His mangled breast was bare.

His face was like the muddy sky
  Before the coming snow;
And dark and dreadful was his eye,
  And cloudy was his brow.

Pale Conrad shrunk, but grasp'd his sword;
  Fear thrill'd in ev'ry vein;
His quiv'ring lip half-spoke its word;
  He paus'd, and shrunk again.

"Pale bloody spectre, at this hour
  Why do'st thou haunt the night?
Has the deep gloomy vault no power
  To keep thee from my sight?

"Why do'st thou glare? Why do'st thou wave
  That fatal cursed knife?
The deed is done, and from the grave
  Who can recall to life?

"Why rolls thine eye beneath thy brow,
  Dark as the midnight storm?
What do'st thou want? O, let me know!
  But hide thy dreadful form.

"I'd give the life's blood from my heart
  To wash my crime away:
If thou'rt a spirit, O, depart!
  Nor haunt a wretch of clay.

"Say, do'st thou with the blessed dwell?
  Return and blessed be!
Or com'st thou from the lowest hell?
  I am more curst than thee."

The form advanc'd with solemn step,
  As though it meant to speak;
And thrice it mov'd its mutt'ring lip,
  But silence did not break.

Then sternly stalk'd with heavy pace,
  Which shook the trembling wall;
And, frowning, turn'd its angry face,
  And vanish'd from the hall.

With fixed eyes, pale Conrad stood,
  That from their sockets swell;
Back on his heart ran the cold blood,

He shudder'd as he fell.

Night fled, and thro' the window 'gan
  The early light to play;
But on a more unhappy man
  Ne'er shone the dawning day.

The gladsome sun all nature cheers,
  But cannot charm his cares:
Still dwells his mind with gloomy fears,
  And murther'd Edward glares.

PART III.

"No rest nor comfort can I find,
  I watch the midnight hour;
I sit and listen to the wind
  Which beats upon my tower.

"Methinks low voices from the ground
  Break mournful on mine ear,
And thro' these empty chambers sound
  So dismal and so drear.

"The ghost of some departed friend
  Doth in my sorrows share;
Or is it but the rushing wind
  That mocketh my despair.

"Sad thro' the hall the pale lamp gleams
  Upon my father's arms:
My soul is fill'd with gloomy dreams,

I fear unknown alarms.

"Oh! I have known this lonely place
  With ev'ry blessing stor'd;
And many a friend with cheerful face
  Sit smiling at my board,

"Whilst round the fire, in early bloom,
  My harmless children play'd,
Who now within the narrow tomb
  Are with their mother laid.

"And now low bends my wretched head,
  And those I lov'd are gone:
My friends, my family, all are fled,
  And I am left alone.

"Oft' as the cheerless fire declines,
  In it I sadly trace,
As 'lone I sit, the half form'd lines
  Of many a much lov'd face.

"But chief, O Marg'ret! to my mind
  Thy lovely features rise:
I strive to think thee less unkind,
  And wipe my streaming eyes.

"For only thee I had to vaunt,
  Thou wert thy mother's pride:
She left thee like a shooting plant
  To screen my widow'd side.

"But thou hast left me weak, forlorn,

And chill'd with age's frost,
To count my weary days, and mourn
  The comforts I have lost.

"Unkindly fair! why did'st thou go?
  O, had I known the truth!
Tho' Edward's father was my foe,
  I would have bless'd the youth.

"O could I see that face again,
  Whose smile calm'd ev'ry strife!
And hear that voice, which sooth'd my pain,
  And made me wish for life!

"Thy harp hangs silent by the wall:
  My nights are sad and long:
And thou art in a distant hall,
  Where strangers raise the song.

"Ha! some delusion of the mind
  My senses doth confound!
It was the harp, and not the wind,
  That did so sweetly sound."

Old Arno rose, all wan as death,
  With broken steps of care;
And oft' he check'd his quick-heav'd breath,
  And turn'd his eager ear.

When like a full, but distant choir
  The swelling sound return'd;
And with the soft and trembling wire,
  The sighing echoes mourn'd.

Then softly whisper'd o'er the song
  Which Marg'ret lov'd to play,
Like some sweet dirge, and sad, and long,
  It faintly died away.

His dim-worn eyes to heav'n he cast,
  Where all his griefs were known;
And smote upon his troubled breast,
  And heav'd a heavy groan.

"I know it is my daughter's hand,
  But 'tis no hand of clay:
And here a lonely wretch I stand,
  All childless, bent, and grey.

"And art thou low, my lovely child?
  And hast thou met thy doom?
And has thy flatt'ring morning smil'd,
  To lead but to the tomb?

"O let me see thee ere we part,
  For souls like thine are blest;
O let me fold thee to my heart
  If aught of form thou hast.

"This passing mist enrobes thy charms:
  Alas, to nought 'tis shrunk!
And hollow strike my empty arms
  Against my aged trunk.

"Thou'rt fled like the low ev'ning breath
  That sighs upon the hill:

O stay! tho' in thy weeds of death,
  Thou art my daughter still."

Loud wak'd the sound, then fainter grew,
  And long and sadly mourn'd;
And softly sigh'd a long adieu,
  And never more return'd.

Old Arno stretch'd him on the ground,
  Thick as the gloom of night,
Death's misty shadows gather'd round,
  And swam before his sight.

He heav'd a deep and deadly groan,
  Which rent his lab'ring breast;
And long before the morning shone,
  His spirit was at rest.

A REVERIE.

  Beside a spreading elm, from whose high boughs
Like knotted tufts the crow's light dwelling shows,
Where screen'd from northern blasts, and winter proof,
Snug stands the parson's barn with thatched roof;
At chaff-strew'd door, where, in the morning ray,
The gilded mots in mazy circles play,
And sleepy Comrade in the sun is laid,
More grateful to the cur than neighb'ring shade;
In snowy shirt unbrac'd, brown Robin stood,
And leant upon his flail in thoughtful mood:
His full round cheek where deeper flushes glow,

The dewy drops which glisten on his brow;
His dark cropt pate that erst at church or fair,
So smooth and silky, shew'd his morning's care,
Which all uncouth in matted locks combin'd,
Now, ends erect, defies the ruffling wind;
His neck-band loose, and hosen rumpled low,
A careful lad, nor slack at labour shew.
Nor scraping chickens chirping 'mongst the straw,
Nor croaking rook o'er-head, nor chatt'ring daw;
Loud-breathing cow amongst the rampy weeds,
Nor grunting sow that in the furrow feeds;
Nor sudden breeze that shakes the quaking leaves,
And lightly rustles thro' the scatter'd sheaves;
Nor floating straw that skims athwart his nose,
The deeply musing youth may discompose.
For Nelly fair, and blythest village maid,
Whose tuneful voice beneath the hedge-row shade,
At early milking, o'er the meadows born,
E'er cheer'd the ploughman's toil at rising morn:
The neatest maid that e'er, in linen gown,
Bore cream and butter to the market town:
The tightest lass, that with untutor'd air
E'er footed ale-house floor at wake or fair,
Since Easter last had Robin's heart possest,
And many a time disturb'd his nightly rest.
Full oft' returning from the loosen'd plough,
He slack'd his pace, and knit his thoughtful brow;
And oft' ere half his thresher's talk was o'er,
Would muse, with arms across, at cooling door:
His mind thus bent, with downcast eyes he stood,
And leant upon his flail in thoughtful mood.
His soul o'er many a soft rememb'rance ran,
And, mutt'ring to himself, the youth began.

"Ah! happy is the man whose early lot
Hath made him master of a furnish'd cot;
Who trains the vine that round his window grows,
And after setting sun his garden hoes;
Whose wattled pales his own enclosure shield,
Who toils not daily in another's field.
Where'er he goes, to church or market town,
With more respect he and his dog are known:
A brisker face he wears at wake or fair,
Nor views with longing eyes the pedlar's ware,
But buys at will or ribands, gloves, or beads,
And willing maidens to the ale-house leads:
And, Oh! secure from toils which cumber life,
He makes the maid he loves an easy wife.
Ah, Nelly! can'st thou with contented mind,
Become the help-mate of a lab'ring hind,
And share his lot, whate'er the chances be,
Who hath no dow'r, but love, to fix on thee?
Yes, gayest maid may meekest matron prove,
And things of little note may 'token love.
When from the church thou cam'st at eventide
And I and red-hair'd Susan by thy side,
I pull'd the blossoms from the bending tree,
And some to Susan gave, and some to thee;
Thine were the best, and well thy smiling eye
The diff'rence mark'd, and guess'd the reason why.
When on a holy-day we rambling stray'd,
And pass'd old Hodge's cottage in the glade;
Neat was the garden dress'd, sweet hum'd the bee,
I wish'd both cot and Nelly made for me;
And well methought thy very eyes reveal'd
The self-same wish within thy breast conceal'd.

When artful, once, I sought my love to tell,
And spoke to thee of one who lov'd thee well,
You saw the cheat, and jeering homeward hied,
Yet secret pleasure in thy looks I spied.
Ay, gayest maid may meekest matron prove,
And smaller signs than these have 'token'd love."

  Now, at a distance, on the neighb'ring plain,
With creaking wheels slow comes the heavy wain:
High on its tow'ring load a maid appears,
And Nelly's voice sounds shrill in Robin's ears.
Quick from his hand he throws the cumb'rous flail,
And leaps with lightsome limbs th' enclosing pale.
O'er field and fence he scours, and furrow wide,
With waken'd Comrade barking by his side;
Whilst tracks of trodden grain, and sidelong hay,
And broken hedge-flow'rs sweet, mark his impetuous way.

A DISAPPOINTMENT.

  On village green, whose smooth and well worn sod,
Cross-path'd with every gossip's foot is trod;
By cottage door where playful children run,
And cats and curs sit basking in the sun:
Where o'er the earthen seat the thorn is bent,
Cross-arm'd, and back to wall, poor William leant.
His bonnet broad drawn o'er his gather'd brow,
His hanging lip and lengthen'd visage shew
A mind but ill at ease. With motions strange,
His listless limbs their wayward postures change;
Whilst many a crooked line and curious maze,

With clouted shoon, he on the sand pourtrays.
The half-chew'd straw fell slowly from his mouth,
And to himself low mutt'ring spoke the youth.

"How simple is the lad! and reft of skill,
Who thinks with love to fix a woman's will:
Who ev'ry Sunday morn, to please her sight,
Knots up his neck-cloth gay, and hosen white:
Who for her pleasure keeps his pockets bare,
And half his wages spends on pedlar's ware;
When every niggard clown, or dotard old,
Who hides in secret nooks his oft told gold,
Whose field or orchard tempts with all her pride,
At little cost may win her for his bride;
Whilst all the meed her silly lover gains
Is but the neighbours' jeering for his pains.
On Sunday last when Susan's bands were read,
And I astonish'd sat with hanging head,
Cold grew my shrinking limbs, and loose my knee,
Whilst every neighbour's eye was fix'd on me.
Ah, Sue! when last we work'd at Hodge's hay,
And still at me you jeer'd in wanton play;
When last at fair, well pleas'd by show-man's stand,
You took the new-bought fairing from my hand;
When at old Hobb's you sung that song so gay,
Sweet William still the burthen of the lay,
I little thought, alas! the lots were cast,
That thou shou'd'st be another's bride at last:
And had, when last we trip'd it on the green
And laugh'd at stiff-back'd Rob, small thought I ween,
Ere yet another scanty month was flown,
To see thee wedded to the hateful clown.
Ay, lucky swain, more gold thy pockets line;

But did these shapely limbs resemble thine,
I'd stay at home, and tend the household geer,
Nor on the green with other lads appear.
Ay, lucky swain, no store thy cottage lacks,
And round thy barn thick stands the shelter'd stacks;
But did such features hard my visage grace,
I'd never budge the bonnet from my face.
Yet let it be: it shall not break my ease:
He best deserves who doth the maiden please.
Such silly cause no more shall give me pain,
Nor ever maiden cross my rest again.
Such grizzly suitors with their taste agree,
And the black fiend may take them all for me!"

  Now thro' the village rise confused sounds,
Hoarse lads, and children shrill, and yelping hounds.
Straight ev'ry matron at the door is seen,
And pausing hedgers on their mattocks lean.
At every narrow lane, and alley mouth,
Loud laughing lasses stand, and joking youth.
A near approaching band in colours gay,
With minstrels blythe before to cheer the way,
From clouds of curling dust which onward fly,
In rural splendour break upon the eye.
As in their way they hold so gayly on,
Caps, beads, and buttons glancing in the sun,
Each village wag, with eye of roguish cast,
Some maiden jogs, and vents the ready jest;
Whilst village toasts the passing belles deride,
And sober matrons marvel at their pride.
But William, head erect, with settled brow,
In sullen silence view'd the passing shew;
And oft' he scratch'd his pate with manful grace,

And scorn'd to pull the bonnet o'er his face;
But did with steady look unmoved wait,
Till hindmost man had turn'd the church-yard gate;
Then turn'd him to his cot with visage flat,
Where honest Tray upon the threshold sat.
Up jump'd the kindly beast his hand to lick,
And, for his pains, receiv'd an angry kick.
Loud shuts the flapping door with thund'ring din;
The echoes round their circling course begin,
From cot to cot, in wide progressive swell,
Deep groans the church-yard wall and neighb'ring dell,
And Tray, responsive, joins with long and piteous yell.

A LAMENTATION.

Where ancient broken wall encloses round,
From tread of lawless feet, the hallow'd ground,
And somber yews their dewy branches wave
O'er many a motey stone and mounded grave:
Where parish church, confus'dly to the sight,
With deeper darkness prints the shades of night,
And mould'ring tombs uncouthly gape around,
And rails and fallen stones bestrew the ground:
In loosen'd garb derang'd, with scatter'd hair,
His bosom open to the nightly air,
Lone, o'er a new heap'd grave poor Basil bent,
And to himself began his simple plaint.

"Alas! how cold thy home! how low thou art!
Who wert the pride and mistress of my heart.
The fallen leaves light rustling o'er thee pass,

And o'er thee waves the rank and dewy grass.
The new laid sods in decent order tell
How narrow now the space where thou must dwell.
Now rough and wint'ry winds may on thee beat,
And drizzly drifting snow, and summer's heat;
Each passing season rub, for woe is me!
Or storm, or sunshine, is the same to thee.
Ah, Mary! lovely was thy slender form,
And sweet thy cheerful brow, that knew no storm.
Thy steps were graceful on the village-green,
As tho' thou had'st some courtly lady been:
At church or market, still the gayest lass,
Each younker slack'd his speed to see thee pass.
At early milking, tuneful was thy lay,
And sweet thy homeward song at close of day;
But sweeter far, and ev'ry youth's desire,
Thy cheerful converse by the ev'ning fire.
Alas! no more thou'lt foot the grassy sward!
No song of thine shall ever more be heard!
Yet now they trip it lightly on the green,
As blythe and gay as thou hadst never been:
The careless younker whittles lightsome by,
And other maidens catch his roving eye:
Around the ev'ning fire, with little care,
The neighbours sit, and scarcely miss thee there;
And when the night advancing darkens round,
They to their rest retire, and slumber sound.
But Basil cannot rest; his days are sad,
And long his nights upon the weary bed.
Yet still in broken dreams thy form appears,
And still my bosom proves a lover's fears.
I guide thy footsteps thro' the tangled wood;
I catch thee sinking in the boist'rous flood;

I shield thy bosom from the threaten'd stroke;
I clasp thee falling from the headlong rock;
But ere we reach the dark and dreadful deep,
High heaves my troubled breast, I wake, and weep.
At ev'ry wailing of the midnight wind
Thy lowly dwelling comes into my mind.
When rain beats on my roof, wild storms abroad,
I think upon thy bare and beaten sod;
I hate the comfort of a shelter'd home,
And hie me forth o'er fenceless fields to roam:
I leave the paths of men for dreary waste,
And bare my forehead to the howling blast.
O Mary! loss of thee hath fix'd my doom:
This world around me is a weary gloom:
Dull heavy musings down my spirits weigh,
I cannot sleep by night, nor work by day.
Or wealth or pleasure slowest minds inspire,
But cheerless is their toil who nought desire.
Let happier friends divide my farmers' dock,
Cut down my grain, and sheer my little flock;
For now my only care on earth shall be
Here ev'ry Sunday morn to visit thee;
And in the holy church, with heart sincere,
And humble mind, our worthy curate hear:
He best can tell, when earthly cares are past,
The surest way to meet with thee at last.
I'll thus a while a weary life abide,
Till wasting Time hath laid me by thy side;
For now on earth there is no place for me,
Nor peace, nor slumber, till I rest with thee."

  Loud, from the lofty spire, with piercing knell,
Solemn, and awful, toll'd the parish bell;

A later hour than rusties deem it meet
That church-yard ground be trode by mortal feet,
The wailing lover startled at the sound,
And rais'd his head and cast his eyes around.
The gloomy pile in strengthen'd horrour lower'd,
Large and majestic ev'ry object tower'd:
Dim thro' the gloom they shew'd their forms unknown,
And tall and ghastly rose each whiten'd stone:
Aloft the waking screech-owl 'gan to sing,
And past him skim'd the bat with flapping wing.
The fears of nature woke within his breast;
He left the hallowed spot of Mary's rest,
And sped his way the church-yard wall to gain,
Then check'd his coward heart, and turn'd again.
The shadows round a deeper horrour wear;
A deeper silence hangs upon his ear;
A stiller rest is o'er the settled scene;
His flutt'ring heart recoils, and shrinks again.
With hasty steps he measures back the ground,
And leaps with summon'd force the church-yard bound;
Then home with knocking limbs, and quicken'd breath,
His footstep urges from the place of death.

AN ADDRESS TO THE MUSES.

Ye tuneful Sifters of the lyre,
Who dreams and fantasies inspire;
Who over poesy preside,
And on a lofty hill abide
Above the ken of mortal fight,
Fain would I sing of you, could I address ye right.

Thus known, your pow'r of old was sung,
And temples with your praises rung;
And when the song of battle rose,
Or kindling wine, or lovers' woes,
The poet's spirit inly burn'd,
And still to you his upcast eyes were turn'd.

The youth all wrapp'd in vision bright,
Beheld your robes of flowing white:
And knew your forms benignly grand,
An awful, but a lovely band;
And felt your inspiration strong,
And warmly pour'd his rapid lay along.

The aged bard all heav'n-ward glow'd,
And hail'd you daughters of a god:
Tho' to his dimmer eyes were seen
Nor graceful form, nor heav'nly mien,
Full well he felt that ye were near,
And heard you in the blast that shook his hoary hair.

Ye lighten'd up the valley's bloom,
And deeper spread the forest's gloom;
The lofty hill sublimer flood,
And grander rose the mighty flood;
For then Religion lent her aid,
And o'er the mind of man your sacred empire spread.

Tho' rolling ages now are past,
And altars low, and temples wade;
Tho' rites and oracles are o'er,
And gods and heros rule no more;

Your fading honours still remain,
And still your vot'ries call, a long and motley train.

They seek you not on hill and plain,
Nor court you in the sacred sane;
Nor meet you in the mid-day dream,
Upon the bank of hallowed stream;
Yet still for inspiration sue,
And still each lifts his fervent prayer to you.

He knows ye not in woodland gloom,
But wooes ye in the shelfed room;
And seeks you in the dusty nook,
And meets you in the letter'd book;
Full well he knows you by your names,
And still with poets faith your presence claims.

The youthful poet, pen in hand,
All by the side of blotted stand,
In rev'rie deep, which none may break,
Sits rubbing of his beardless cheek;
And well his inspiration knows,
E'en by the dewy drops that trickle o'er his nose.

The tuneful sage of riper fame,
Perceives you not in heated frame;
But at conclusion of his verse,
Which still his mutt'ring lips rehearse,
Oft' waves his hand in grateful pride,
And owns the heav'nly pow'r that did his fancy guide.

O lovely sisters! is it true,
That they are all inspir'd by you?

And while they write, with magic charm'd,
And high enthusiasm warm'd,
We may not question heav'nly lays,
For well I wot, they give you all the praise.

O lovely sisters! well it shews
How wide and far your bounty flows:
Then why from me withhold your beams?
Unvisited of heav'nly dreams,
Whene'er I aim at heights sublime,
Still downward am I call'd to seek some stubborn rhyme.

No hasty lightning breaks the gloom,
Nor flashing thoughts unsought for come,
Nor fancies wake in time of need;
I labour much with little speed;
And when my studied task is done,
Too well, alas! I mark it for my own.

Yet should you never smile on me,
And rugged still my verses be;
Unpleasing to the tuneful train,
Who only prize a slowing strain;
And still the learned scorn my lays,
I'll lift my heart to you, and sing your praise.

Your varied ministry to trace,
Your honour'd names, and godlike race;
And lofty bow'rs where fountains flow,
They'll better sing who better know;
I praise ye not with Grecian lyre,
Nor will I hail ye daughters of a heathen fire.

Ye are the spirits who preside
In earth, and air, and ocean wide;
In hissing flood, and crackling fire;
In horror dread, and tumult dire;
In stilly calm, and stormy wind,
And rule the answ'ring changes in the human mind.

High on the tempest-beaten hill,
Your misty shapes ye shift at will;
The wild fantastic clouds ye form;
Your voice is in the midnight storm;
Whilst in the dark and lonely hour,
Oft' starts the boldest heart, and owns your secret pow'r.

From you, when growling storms are past,
And light'ning ceases on the wade,
And when the scene of blood is o'er,
And groans of death are heard no more,
Still holds the mind each parted form,
Like after echoing of the o'erpassed storm.

When closing glooms o'erspread the day,
And what we love has pass'd away,
Ye kindly bid each pleasing scene
Within the bosom still remain,
Like moons who doth their watches run
With the reflected brightness of the parted sun.

The shining day, and nightly shade,
The cheerful plain and gloomy glade,
The homeward flocks, and shepherds play,
The busy hamlet's closing day,
Full many a breast with pleasures swell,

Who ne'er shall have the gift of words to tell,

Oft' when the moon looks from on high,
And black around the shadows lie;
And bright the sparkling waters gleam,
And rushes rustle by the stream,
Shrill sounds, and fairy forms are known
By simple 'nighted swains, who wander late alone.

Ye kindle up the inward glow,
Ye strengthen ev'ry outward show;
Ye overleap the strongest bar,
And join what Nature sunders far:
And visit oft' in fancies wild,
The bread of learned sage, and simple child.

From him who wears a monarch's crown,
To the unletter'd artless clown,
All in some strange and lonely hour
Have felt, unsought, your secret pow'r,
And lov'd your roving fancies well,
You add but to the bard the art to tell.

Ye mighty spirits of the song,
To whom the poets' pray'rs belong,
My lowly bosom to inspire,
And kindle with your sacred fire,
Your wild obscuring heights to brave,
Is boon, alas! too great for me to crave.

But O, such sense of matter bring!
As they who feel and never sing
Wear on their hearts, it will avail

With simple words to tell my tale;
And still contented will I be,
Tho' greater inspirations never fall to me.

A MELANCHOLY LOVER'S FAREWELL TO HIS MISTRESS.

My Phillis, all my hopes are o'er,
And I shall see thy face no more.
Since ev'ry secret wish is vain,
I will not stay to give thee pain.
Then do not hang thy low'ring brow,
But let me bless thee ere I go:
Nor, O, despise my last adieu!
I've lov'd thee long, and lov'd thee true.

The prospects of my youth are crost,
My health is flown, my vigour lost;
My soothing friends augment my pain,
And cheerless is my native plain;
Dark o'er my spirit hangs the gloom,
And thy disdain has fix'd my doom.
But light gales ruffle o'er the sea,
Which soon shall bear me far from thee;
And wherefoe'er our course is cast,
I know will bear me to my rest.
Full deep beneath the briny wave,
Where rest the venturous and brave,
A place may be decreed for me;
And should no tempest raise the sea,

Far hence upon a foreign land,
Whose sons, perhaps, with friendly hand
The stranger's lowly tomb may raise;
A broken heart will end my days.

But Heaven's blessing on thee rest!
And may no troubles vex thy breast!
Perhaps, when pensive and alone,
You'll think of me when I am gone;
And gentle tears of pity shed,
When I am in my narrow bed.
Yet softly let thy sorrow flow!
And greater may'st thou never know!
All free from worldly care and strife,
Long may'ft thou live a happy life!
And ev'ry earthly blessing find,
Thou loveliest of womankind:
And blest thy secret wishes be!
Tho' cruel thou hast been to me.

And do'st thou then thine arm extend
And may I take thy lovely hand?
And do thine eyes thus gently look,
As tho' some kindly wish they spoke?
My gentle Phillis, tho' severe,
I do not grudge the ills I bear;
But still my greatest grief will be,
To think my love has troubled thee.
O, do not scorn this swelling grief!
The laden bosom seeks relief:
Nor yet this infant weakness blame,
For thou hast made me what I am.
But hark! the sailors call away,

No longer may I ling'ring stay;
May peace within thy mansion dwell!
O, gentle Phillis, fare thee well!

A CHEERFUL TEMPERED LOVER'S FAREWELL TO HIS MISTRESS.

The light winds on the streamers play
That soon shall bear me far away;
My comrades give the parting cheer,
And I alone have linger'd here.
Now Phill. my love, since it will be,
And I must bid farewell to thee,
Since ev'ry hope of thee is flown,
Ne'er send me from thee with a frown;
But let me kindly take thy hand,
And bid God bless me in a foreign land.

No more I'll loiter by thy side,
Well pleas'd thy gamesome taunts to bide;
Nor lovers' gambols lightly try
To make me graceful in thine eye;
Nor sing the merry roundelay,
To cheer thee at the close of day.
Yet ne'ertheless tho' we must part,
I'll bear thee still upon my heart;
And oft' I'll fill the ruddy glass,
To toast my lovely scornful lass.
Far hence, upon a foreign shore,
Still will I keep an open door,

And still my little fortune share
With all who ever breath'd my native air.
And who thy beauteous face hath seen,
Or ever near thy dwelling been,
Shall push about the flowing bowl,
And be the matter of the whole.
And ev'ry woman for thy sake,
Though proud and cruel, as they're weak,
Shall in my walls protection find,
Thou fairest of a fickle kind.

  O, dearly! dearly! have I paid,
Thou little haughty cruel maid,
To give that inward peace to thee,
Which thou hast ta'en away from me.
Soft hast thou slept, with bosom light,
Whilst I have watch'd the weary night;
And now I cross the surgy deep,
That thou may'st still untroubled sleep--
But in thine eyes, what do I see,
That looks as tho' they pitied me?
I thank thee, Phill. yet be not sad,
I leave no blame upon thy head.
I would, more grac'd with pleasing make,
I had been better for thy sake,
But yet, perhaps, when I shall dwell
Far hence, thou'lt sometimes think how well--
I dare not stay, since we must part,
T'expose a fond and foolish heart;
Where'er I go, it beats for you,
God bless ye, Phill. adieu! adieu!

A PROUD LOVER'S FAREWELL TO HIS MISTRESS.

   Farewell thou haughty, cruel fair!
Upon thy brow no longer wear
That sombre look of cold disdain,
Thou ne'er shalt see my face again.
Now ev'ry silly wish is o'er,
And fears and doubtings are no more.

   All cruel as thou art to me,
Long has my heart been fix'd on thee;
On thee I've mus'd the live-long day,
And thought the weary night away;
I've trac'd thy footsteps o'er the green,
And shar'd thy rambles oft unseen;
I've linger'd near thee night and day,
When thou hast thought me far away;
I've watch'd the turning of thy face,
And fondly mark'd thy moving grace;
And wept thy rising smiles to see;
I've been a fool for love of thee.
Yet do not think I stay the while
Thy weakly pity to beguile:
Let forced favour fruitless prove!
The pity curst, that brings not love!
No woman e'er shall give me pain,
Or ever break my rest again:
Nor aught that comes of woman kind
Have pow'r again to move my mind.
Far on a foreign shore I'll seek
Some lonely island, bare and bleak;
I'll seek some wild and rugged cell,

And with untamed creatures dwell.
To hear their cries is now my choice,
Far more than man's deceitful voice:
To listen to the howling wind,
Than luring tongue of womankind.
They look not beautiful and good,
But ronghsome seem as they are rude.

  O Phillis! thou hast wreck'd a heart,
Which proudly bears, but feels the smart.
Adieu! adieu! should'st thou e'er prove
The pang of ill-requited love,
Thou'lt know what I have borne for thee,
And then thou wilt remember me.

A POET, OR, SOUND-HEARTED LOVER'S FAREWELL TO HIS MISTRESS.

  Fair Nymph, who dost my fate controul,
And reign'st the mistress of my soul,
Where thou all bright in beauties ray
Hast held a long tyrannick sway,
They who the hardest rule maintain,
In their commands do still refrain
From what impossible must prove,
But thou hast bade me cease to love;
Nor would some gentle mercy give,
And only bid me cease to live.
Ah! when the magnet's pow'r is o'er,
The compass then will point no more;

And when no verdure cloaths the spring,
The tuneful birds forget to sing:
But thou all sweet and heav'nly fair,
Hast bade thy swain from love forbear.
In pity let thine own fair hand
A death's-wound to this bosom send:
This tender heart of purest faith
May then resign thee with its breath;
And in the sun-beam of thine eye
A proud and willing victim die.

  But since thou wilt not have it so,
Far from thy presence will I go:
Far from my heart's dear bliss I'll stray,
Since I no longer can obey.
In foreign climes I'll distant roam,
No more to hail my native home:
To foreign swains I'll pour my woe,
In foreign plains my tears shall flow:
By murm'ring stream and shady grove
Shall other echoes tell my love;
And richer flow'rs of vivid hue
Upon my tomb shall other maidens strew.

  Adieu, dear Phillis! should'ft thou e'er
Some soft and plaintive story hear,
Of hapless youth who died for love,
Or all forlorn did banish'd rove,
O think of me! nor then deny
The gentle tribute of a sigh.

     *   *   *   *   *

It may be objected that all these lovers are equally sad, though one is a cheerful, the other a melancholy lover. It is true they are all equally sad, for they are all equally in love, and in despair, when it is impossible for them to be otherwise; but if I have pictured their farewell complaints in such a way as to give you an idea that one lover is naturally of a melancholy, one of a cheerful, and one of a proud temper, I have done all that is intended.

THE STORM-BEAT MAID.

SOMEWHAT AFTER THE STYLE OF OUR OLD ENGLISH BALLADS.

All shrouded in the winter snow,
  The maiden held her way;
Nor chilly winds that roughly blow,
  Nor dark night could her stay.

O'er hill and dale, through bush and briar,
  She on her journey kept;
Save often when she 'gan to tire,
  She stop'd awhile and wept.

Wild creatures left their caverns drear,
  To raise their nightly yell;
But little doth the bosom fear,
  Where inward troubles dwell.

No watch-light from the distant spire,
  To cheer the gloom so deep,
Nor twinkling star, nor cottage fire

Did thro' the darkness peep.

Yet heedless still she held her way,
  Nor fear'd the crag nor dell;
Like ghost that thro' the gloom to stray,
  Wakes with the midnight bell.

Now night thro' her dark watches ran,
  Which lock the peaceful mind;
And thro' the neighb'ring hamlets 'gan
  To wake the yawning hind.

Yet bark of dog, nor village cock,
  That spoke the morning near;
Nor gray-light trembling on the rock,
  Her 'nighted mind could cheer.

The whirling flail, and clacking mill
  Wake with the early day;
And careless children, loud and shrill,
  With new-made snow-balls play.

And as she pass'd each cottage door,
  They did their gambols cease;
And old men shook their locks so hoar,
  And wish'd her spirit peace.

For sometimes slow; and sometimes fast,
  She held her wav'ring pace;
Like early spring's inconstant blast,
  That ruffles evening's face.

At length with weary feet she came,

Where in a shelt'ring wood,
Whose master bore no humble name,
  A stately castle stood.

The open gate, and smoking fires,
  Which cloud the air so thin;
And shrill bell tinkling from the spires,
  Bespoke a feast within.

With busy looks, and hasty tread,
  The servants cross the hall;
And many a page, in buskins red,
  Await the master's call.

Fair streaming bows of bridal white
  On ev'ry shoulder play'd;
And clean, in lily kerchief dight,
  Trip'd every houshold maid.

She ask'd for neither lord nor dame,
  Nor who the mansion own'd;
But straight into the hall she came,
  And sat her on the ground.

The busy crew all crouded nigh,
  And round the stranger star'd;
But still she roll'd her wand'ring eye,
  Nor for their questions car'd.

"What dost thou want, thou storm-beat' maid,
  That thou these portals past?
Ill suiteth here thy looks dismay'd,
  Thou art no bidden guest."

"O chide not!" said a gentle page,
  And wip'd his tear-wet cheek,
"Who would not shun the winter's rage?
  The wind is cold and bleak.

"Her robe is stiff with drizly snow,
  And rent her mantle grey;
None ever bade the wretched go
  Upon his wedding-day."

Then to his lord he hied him straight,
  Where round on silken seat
Sat many a courteous dame and knight.
  And made obeisance meet,

"There is a stranger in your hall,
  Who wears no common mien;
Hard were the heart, as flinty wall,
  That would not take her in.

"A fairer dame in hall or bower
  Mine eyes did ne'er behold;
Tho' shelter'd in no father's tower,
  And turn'd out to the cold.

"Her face is like an early morn,
  Dimm'd with the nightly dew;
Her skin is like the sheeted torn,
  Her eyes are wat'ry blue.

"And tall and slender is her form,
  Like willow o'er the brook;

But on her brow there broods a storm,
  And restless is her look,

"And well her troubled motions shew
  The tempest in her mind;
Like the unshelter'd sapling bough
  Vex'd with the wintry wind.

"Her head droops on her ungirt breast,
  And scatter'd is her hair;
Yet lady brac'd in courtly vest
  Was never half so fair."

Reverse, and cold the turning blood
  The bridegroom's cheek forsook:
He shook and stagger'd as he stood,
  And falter'd as he spoke.

"So soft and fair I know a maid,
  There is but only she;
A wretched man her love betrayed,
  And wretched let him be."

Deep frowning, turn'd the bride's dark eye,
  For bridal morn unmeet;
With trembling steps her lord did hie
  The stranger fair to greet.

Tho' loose in scatter'd weeds array'd,
  And ruffled with the storm;
Like lambkin from its fellows stray'd,
  He knew her graceful form.

But when he spy'd her sunken eye,
  And features sharp and wan,
He heav'd a deep and heavy sigh,
  And down the big tears ran.

"Why droops thy head, thou lovely maid,
  Upon thy hand of snow?
Is it because thy love betray'd,
  That thou art brought so low?"

Quick from her eye the keen glance came
  Who question'd her to see:
And oft she mutter'd o'er his name,
  And wist not it was he.

Full hard against his writhing brows
  His clenched hands he prest;
Full high his lab'ring bosom rose,
  And rent its silken vest.

"O cursed be the golden price,
  That did my baseness prove!
And cursed be my friends advice,
  That wil'd me from thy love!

"And cursed be the woman's art,
  That lur'd me to her snare!
And cursed be the faithless heart
  That left thee to despair!

"Yet now I'll hold thee to my side,
  Tho' worthless I have been,
Nor friends, nor wealth, nor dizen'd bride,

Shall ever stand between.

"When thou art weary and depress'd,
 I'll lull thee to thy sleep;
And when dark fancies vex thy breast,
 I'll sit by thee and weep.

"I'll tend thee like a restless child
 Where'er thy rovings be;
Nor gesture keen, nor eye-ball wild,
 Shall turn my love from thee.

"Night shall not hang cold o'er thy head,
 And I securely lie;
Nor drizly clouds upon thee shed,
 And I in covert dry.

"I'll share the cold blast on the heath,
 I'll share thy wants and pain:
Nor friend nor foe, nor life nor death,
 Shall ever make us twain."

THUNDER.

Spirit of strength, to whom in wrath 'tis given
To mar the earth, and shake the vasty heaven:
Behold the gloomy robes, that spreading hide
Thy secret majesty, lo! slow and wide,
Thy heavy skirts sail in the middle air,
Thy sultry shroud is o'er the noonday glare:
Th' advancing clouds sublimely roll'd on high,

Deep in their pitchy volumes clothe the sky;
Like hosts of gath'ring foes array'd in death,
Dread hangs their gloom upon the earth beneath,
It is thy hour: the awful deep is still,
And laid to rest the wind of ev'ry hill.
Wild creatures of the forest homeward scour,
And in their dens with fear unwonted cow'r.
Pride in the lordly palace is forgot,
And in the lowly shelter of the cot
The poor man sits, with all his fam'ly round,
In awful expectation of thy sound.
Lone on his way the trav'ller stands aghast;
The fearful looks of man to heav'n are cast,
When, lo! thy lightning gleams on high,
As swiftly turns his startled eye;
And swiftly as thy shooting blaze
Each half performed motion stays,
Deep awe, all human strife and labour stills,
And thy dread voice alone, the earth and heaven fills.

  Bright bursts the lightning from the cloud's dark womb,
As quickly swallow'd in the closing gloom.
The distant streamy flashes, spread askance
In paler sheetings, skirt the wide expanse.
Dread flaming from aloft, the cat'ract dire
Oft meets in middle space the nether fire.
Fierce, red, and ragged, shiv'ring in the air,
Athwart mid-darkness shoots the lengthen'd glare.
Wild glancing round, the feebler lightning plays;
The rifted centre pours the gen'ral blaze;
And from the warring clouds in fury driven[1],

---

1 In poetry we have only to do with appearances; and the
    zig-zag lightning, commonly thought to be the thunder-bolt, is certainly

Red writhing falls the keen embodied bolt of heaven.

  From the dark bowels of the burthen'd cloud
Dread swells the rolling peal, full, deep'ning, loud.
Wide ratt'ling claps the heavens scatter'd o'er,
In gathered strength lift the tremendous roar;
With weaning force it rumbles over head,
Then, growling, wears away to silence dread.
Now waking from afar in doubled might,
Slow rolling onward to the middle height;
Like crash of mighty mountains downward hurl'd,
Like the upbreaking of a wrecking world,
In dreadful majesty, th' explosion grand
Bursts wide, and awful, o'er the trembling land.
The lofty mountains echo back the roar,
Deep from afar rebounds earth's rocky shore;
All else existing in the senses bound
Is lost in the immensity of sound.
Wide jarring sounds by turns in strength convene,
And deep, and terrible, the solemn pause between.

  Aloft upon the mountain's side
The kindled forest blazes wide.
Huge fragments of the rugged deep
Are tumbled to the lashing deep.
Firm rooted in the cloven rock,
Loud crashing falls the stubborn oak.
The lightning keen, in wasteful ire,
Fierce darting on the lofty spire,
Wide rends in twain the ir'n-knit stone,
And stately tow'rs are lowly thrown.

---

firm and embodied, compared to the ordinary lightning, which takes no
distinct shape at all.

Wild flames o'erscour the wide campaign,
And plough askance the hissing main.
Nor strength of man may brave the storm,
Nor shelter skreen the shrinking form;
Nor castle wall its fury stay,
Nor masy gate may bar its way.
It visits those of low estate,
It shakes the dwellings of the great,
It looks athwart the secret tomb,
And glares upon the prison's gloom;
While dungeons deep, in unknown light,
Flash hidious on the wretches' fight,
And lowly groans the downward cell,
Where deadly silence wont to dwell.

Now upcast eyes to heav'n adore,
And knees that never bow'd before.
In stupid wonder flares the child;
The maiden turns her glances wild,
And lifts to hear the coming roar:
The aged shake their locks so hoar:
And stoutest hearts begin to fail,
And many a manly cheek is pale;
Till nearer closing peals astound,
And crashing ruin mingles round;
Then 'numbing fear awhile up-binds
The pausing action of their minds,
Till wak'd to dreadful sense, they lift their eyes,
And round the stricken corse, shrill shrieks of horror rise.

Now thinly spreads the falling hall
A motly winter o'er the vale,
The hailstones bounding as they fall

On hardy rock, or storm-beat' wall.
The loud beginning peal its fury checks,
Now full, now fainter, with irreg'lar breaks,
Then weak in force, unites the scatter'd found;
And rolls its lengthen'd grumblings to the distant bound.
A thick and muddy whiteness clothes the sky,
In paler flashes gleams the lightning by;
And thro' the rent cloud, silver'd with his ray,
The sun looks down on all this wild affray;
As high enthron'd above all mortal ken,
A greater Pow'r beholds the strife of men:
Yet o'er the distant hills the darkness scowls,
And deep, and long, the parting tempest growls.

WIND.

Pow'r uncontrollable, who hold'st thy sway
In the unbounded air, whose trackless way
Is in the firmament, unknown of fight,
Who bend'st the sheeted heavens in thy might,
And lift'st the ocean from its lowest bed
To join in middle space the conflict dread;
Who o'er the peopled earth in ruin scours,
And buffets the firm rock that proudly low'rs,
Thy signs are in the heav'ns. The upper clouds
Draw shapeless o'er the sky their misty shrouds;
Whilst darker fragments rove in lower bands,
And mournful purple cloaths the distant lands.
In gather'd tribes, upon the hanging peak
The sea-fowl scream, ill-omen'd creatures shriek:
Unwonted sounds groan on the distant wave,

And murmurs deep break from the downward cave.
Unlook'd-for gusts the quiet forests shake,
And speak thy coming--awful Pow'r, awake!

  Like burst of mighty waters wakes the blast,
In wide and boundless sweep: thro' regions vast
The floods of air in loosen'd fury drive,
And meeting currents strong, and fiercely strive.
First wildly raving on the mountain's brow
'Tis heard afar, till o'er the plains below
With even rushing force it bears along,
And gradual swelling, louder, full, and strong,
Breaks wide in scatter'd bellowing thro' the air.
Now is it hush'd to calm, now rous'd to war,
Whilst in the pauses of the nearer blast,
The farther gusts howl from the distant waste.
Now rushing furious by with loosen'd sweep,
Now rolling grandly on, solemn and deep,
Its bursting strength the full embodied sound
In wide and shallow brawlings scatters round;
Then wild in eddies shrill, with rage distraught,
And force exhausted, whistles into naught.
With growing might, arising in its room,
From far, like waves of ocean onward come
Succeeding gusts, and spend their wasteful ire,
Then slow, in grumbled mutterings retire:
And solemn stillness overawes the land,
Save where the tempest growls along the distant strand.
But great in doubled strength, afar and wide,
Returning battle wakes on ev'ry side;
And rolling on with full and threat'ning sound,
In wildly mingled fury closes round.
With bellowings loud, and hollow deep'ning swell,

Reiterated hiss, and whistlings shrill,
Fierce wars the varied storm, with fury tore,
Till all is overwhelm'd in one tremendous roar.

  The vexed forest, tossing wide,
Uprooted strews its fairest pride;
The lofty pine in twain is broke,
And crushing falls the knotted oak.
The huge rock trembles in its might;
The proud tow'r tumbles from its height;
Uncover'd stands the social home;
High rocks aloft the city dome;
Whilst bursting bar, and flapping gate,
And crashing roof, and clatt'ring grate,
And hurling wall, and falling spire,
Mingle in jarring din and ruin dire.
Wild ruin scours the works of men;
Their motly fragments strew the plain.
E'en in the desert's pathless waste,
Uncouth destruction marks the blast:
And hollow caves whose secret pride,
Grotesque and grand, was never ey'd
By mortal man, abide its drift,
Of many a goodly pillar reft.
Fierce whirling mounts the desert sand,
And threats aloft the peopl'd land.
The great expanded ocean, heaving wide,
Rolls to the farthest bound its lashing tide;
Whilst in the middle deep afar are seen,
All stately from the sunken gulfs between,
The tow'ring waves, which bend with hoary brow,
Then dash impetuous to the deep below.
With broader sweepy base, in gather'd might

Majestic, swelling to stupendous height,
The mountain billow lifts its awful head,
And, curving, breaks aloft with roarings dread.
Sublimer still the mighty waters rise,
And mingle in the strife of nether skies.
All wildness and uproar, above, beneath,
A world immense of danger, dread, and death.

In dumb despair the sailor stands,
The frantic merchant wrings his hands,
Advent'rous hope clings to the yard,
And sinking wretches shriek unheard:
Whilst on the land, the matron ill at rest,
Thinks of the distant main, and heaves her heavy breast.
The peasants leave their ruin'd home,
And o'er the fields distracted roam:
Insensible the 'numbed infant sleeps,
And helpless bending age, weak and unshelter'd weeps.
Low shrinking fear, in place of state,
Skulks in the dwellings of the great.
The rich man marks with careful eye,
Each wasteful gust that whistles by;
And ill men fear'd with fancied screams
Sit list'ning to the creaking beams.
At break of ev'ry rising squall
On storm-beat' roof, or ancient wall,
Full many a glance of fearful eye
Is upward cast, till from on high,
From cracking joist, and gaping rent,
And falling fragments warning sent,
Loud wakes around the wild affray,
'Tis all confusion and dismay.

Now powerful but inconstant in its course,
The tempest varies with uncertain force.
Like doleful wailings on the lonely waste,
Solemn and dreary sounds the weaning blast.
Exhausted gusts recoiling growl away,
And, wak'd anew, return with feebler sway;
Save where between the ridgy mountains pent,
The fierce imprison'd current strives for vent,
With hollow howl, and lamentation deep,
Then rushes o'er the plain with partial sweep.
A parting gust o'erscours the weary land,
And lowly growls along the distant strand:
Light thro' the wood the shiv'ring branches play,
And on the ocean far it slowly dies away.

AN ADDRESS TO THE NIGHT.

A FEARFUL MIND.

Uncertain, awful as the gloom of death,
The Night's grim shadows cover all beneath.
Shapeless and black is ev'ry object round,
And lost in thicker gloom the distant bound.
Each swelling height is clad with dimmer shades,
And deeper darkness marks the hollow glades.
The moon in heavy clouds her glory veils,
And slow along their passing darkness sails;
While lesser clouds in parted fragments roam,
And red stars glimmer thro' the river's gloom.

Nor cheerful voice is heard from man's abode,

Nor sounding footsteps on the neighb'ring road;
Nor glimm'ring fire the distant cottage tells;
On all around a fearful stillness dwells:
The mingled noise of industry is laid,
And silence deepens with the nightly shade.
Though still the haunts of men, and shut their light,
Thou art not silent, dark mysterious Night,
The cries of savage creatures wildly break
Upon thy quiet; birds ill-omen'd shriek;
Commotions strange disturb the rustling trees;
And heavy plaints come on the passing breeze.
Far on the lonely waste, and distant way,
Unwonted sounds are heard, unknown of day.
With shrilly screams the haunted cavern rings;
And heavy treading of unearthly things
Sounds loud and hollow thro' the ruin'd dome;
Yea, voices issue from the secret tomb.

   But lo! a sudden flow of bursting light!
What wild surrounding scenes break on the sight!
Huge rugged rocks uncouthly low'r on high,
Whilst on the plain their lengthen'd shadows lie.
The wooded banks in streamy brightness glow;
And waving darkness skirts the flood below.
The roving shadow hastens o'er the stream;
And like a ghost's pale shroud the waters glean.
Black fleeting shapes across the valley stray:
Gigantic forms tow'r on the distant way:
The sudden winds in wheeling eddies change:
'Tis all confus'd, unnatural, and strange.
Now all again in horrid gloom is lost:
Wild wakes the breeze like sound of distant host:
Bright shoots along the swift returning light:

Succeeding shadows close the startled sight.
Some restless spirit holds the nightly sway:
Long is the wild, and doubtful is my way.
Inconstant Night, whate'er thy changes be,
It suits not man to be alone with thee.
O! for the shelt'ring roof of lowest kind,
Secure to rest with others of my hind!

AN ADDRESS TO THE NIGHT.

A DISCONTENTED MIND.

How thick the clouds of night are rang'd o'er head!
Confounding darkness o'er the earth is spread.
The clouded moon her cheering count'nance hides;
And feeble stars, between the ragged sides
Of broken clouds, with unavailing ray,
Look thro' to mock the trav'ller on his way.
Tree, bush, and rugged rock, and hollow dell,
In deeper shades their forms confus'dly tell,
To cheat the weary wand'rer's doubtful eye;
Whilst chilly passing winds come ruffling by;
And tangled briars perplex the darken'd pass;
And slimy reptiles glimmer on the grass;
And stinging night-flies spend their cursed spite;
Unhospitable are thy shades, O Night!

Now hard suspicion bars the creaking door;
And safe within the selfish worldlings snore:
And wealthy fools are warm in downy bed:
And houseless beggars shelter in the shed:

And nestling coveys cow'r beneath the brake;
While prowling mischief only is awake.
Each hole and den fends forth its cursed brood,
And savage bloody creatures range the wood.
The thievish vagrant plies his thriftless trade
Beneath the friendly shelter of the shade;
Whilst boldest risk the lawless robber braves:
The day for fools was made, and night for knaves.

  O welcome, kindly moon! thy light display,
And guide a weary trav'ller on his way.
Hill, wood, and valley, brighten in her beam;
And wavy silver glitters on the stream.
The distant path-way shews distinct and clear,
From far inviting, but perplex'd when near.
For blackning shadows add deceitful length,
And lesser objects gain unwonted strength;
Each step misguiding; to the eye unknown,
The shining gutter, from the glist'ning stone;
While crossing shadows checker o'er the ground,
The more perplexing for the brightness round.
Deceitful are thy smiles, untoward Night!
Thy gloom is better than misguiding light.
Then welcome is yon cloud that onward fails,
And all this glary shew in darkness veils.
But see how soon the fleeting shade is past,
And streamy brightness moots across the waste.
Now fly the shadows borne upon the wind;
Succeeding brightness travels fast behind.
And now it low'rs again. Inconstant Night,
Confound thy freaks! be either dark or light.
Yet let them come; whate'er thy changes be,
I was a fool to put my trust in thee.

AN ADDRESS TO THE NIGHT.

A SORROWFUL MIND.

How lone and dreary hangs the sombre Night
O'er wood and valley, stream and craggy height!
While nearer objects, bush, and waving bough,
Their dark uncertain forms but dimly show;
Like those with which disturbed fancies teem,
And shape the scen'ry of a gloomy dream.
The moon is cover'd with her sable shrowd;
And o'er the heav'us rove many a dusky cloud;
Thro' ragged rents the paly sky is seen,
And feebly glance the twinkling stars between:
Whilst earth below is wrapt in stilly gloom,
All sad and silent as the closed tomb.

No bleating flock is heard upon the vale;
Nor lowing kine upon the open dale;
Nor voice of hunter on the lonely heath;
Nor sound of trav'ller on the distant path.
Shut is the fenced door of man's abode;
And ruffling breezes only are abroad.
How mournful is thy voice, O nightly gale!
Across the wood, or down the narrow vale;
And sad, tho' secret and unknown they be,
The sighs of woeful hearts that wake with thee.
For now no friends the haunts of sorrow seek;
Tears hang unchidden on the mourner's cheek:
No side-look vexes from the curious eye;

Nor calm reproving reasoner is by;
The kindly cumbrous visitor is gone,
And laden spirits love to sigh alone.
O Night! wild sings the wind, deep low'rs the shade;
Thy robe is gloomy, and thy voice is sad:
But weary souls confin'd in earthly cell
Are deep in kindred gloom, and love thee well.

But now the veiling darkness passes by;
The moon unclouded holds the middle sky.
A soft and mellow light is o'er the wood;
And silv'ry pureness sparkles on the flood.
White tow'r the clifts from many a craggy breach;
The brown heath shews afar its dreary stretch.
While fairer as the brighten'd object swells,
Fast by its side the darker shadow dwells:
The lofty mountains form the deeper glade,
And keener light but marks the blacker made.
Then welcome yonder clouds that swiftly sail,
And o'er yon glary op'ning draw the veil.
But, ah! too swiftly flies the friendly shade!
Returning brightness travels up the glade,
And all is light again. O fickle Night!
No traveller is here to bless thy light.
I seek nor home, nor shed; I have no way;
Why send thy beams to one who cannot stray?
Or wood, or desert, is the same to me;
O low'r again, and let me rest with thee!

AN ADDRESS TO THE NIGHT.

A JOYFUL MIND.

The warping gloom of night is gather'd round;
And varied darkness marks the uneven ground.
A dimmer shade is on the mountain's brow,
And deeper low'rs the lengthen'd vale below;
While nearer objects all enlarged and dark,
Their strange and shapeless forms uncouthly mark;
Which thro' muddy night are dimly shown,
Like old companions in a garb unknown.
The heavy sheeted clouds are spread on high,
And streaky darkness bounds the farther sky:
And swift along the lighter vagrants sweep,
Whilst clear stars thro' their riven edges peep.
Soft thro' each ragged breach, and streamy rent,
And open gaps in dusky circle pent,
The upper heaven looks serenely bright
In dappled gold, and snowy fleeces dight:
And on the middle current lightly glides
The lesser cloud, with silver wreathy sides.
In sudden gusts awakes the nightly breeze
Across the wood, and rustles thro' the trees;
Or whistles on the plain with eddying sweep;
Or issues from the glen in wailings deep,
Which die away upon the open vale:
Whilst in the pauses of the ruffling gale
The buzzing night-fly rises from the ground,
And wings his flight in many a mazy round;
And lonely owls begin their nightly strain,

So hateful to the ear of 'nighted swain.
Thou do'st the weary trav'ller mislead;
Thy voice is roughsome, and uncooth thy weed,
O gloomy Night! for black thy shadows be,
And fools have rais'd a bad report on thee.
Yet art thou free and friendly to the gay,
And light hearts prize thee equal to the day.

 Now tiresome plodding folks are gone to rest;
And soothing slumber locks the careful breast.
And tell-tale friends, and wise advisers snore;
And softly slip-shod youths unbar the door.
Now footsteps echo far, and watch-dogs bark;
Worms glow, and cats' eyes glitter in the dark.
The vagrant lover crosses moor and hill,
And near the lowly cottage whistles shrill:
Or, bolder grown, beneath the friendly shade,
Taps at the window of his fav'rite maid;
Who from above his simple tale receives,
Whilst stupid matrons start, and think of thieves,
Now daily fools unbar the narrow soul,
All wise and gen'rous o'er the nightly bowl.
The haunted wood receives its motley host,
(By trav'ller shun'd) tho' neither fag nor ghost;
And there the crackling bonfire blazes red,
While merry vagrants feast beneath the shed.
From sleepless beds unquiet spirits rise,
And cunning wags put on their borrow'd guise:
Whilst silly maidens mutter o'er their boon,
And crop their fairy weeds beneath the moon:
And harmless plotters slyly take the road,
And trick and playful mischief is abroad.

But, lo! the moon looks forth in splendour bright,
Fair and unclouded, from her middle height.
The passing cloud unveils her kindly ray,
And slowly sails its weary length away;
While broken fragments from its fleecy side,
In dusky bands before it swiftly glide;
Their misty texture changing with the wind,
A strange and scatter'd group, of motley kind
As ever earth or fruitful ocean fed,
Or ever youthful poets fancy bred.
His surgy length the wreathing serpent trails,
And by his side the rugged camel sails:
The winged griffith follows close behind,
And spreads his dusky pinions to the wind.
Athwart the sky in scatter'd bands they range
From shape to shape, transform'd in endless change;
Then piece meal torn, in ragged portions stray,
Or thinly spreading, slowly melt away.
A softer brightness covers all below;
Hill, dale, and wood, in mellow'd colour's glow.
High tow'rs the whiten'd rock in added strength;
The brown heath shews afar its dreary length.
The winding river glitters on the vale;
And gilded trees wave in the passing gale.
Upon the ground each black'ning shadow lies,
And hasty darkness o'er the valley flies.
Wide sheeting shadows travel o'er the plain,
And swiftly close upon the varied scene.
Return, O lovely moon! and look from high,
All stately riding in thy motled sky,
Yet, O thy beams in hasty visits come!
As swiftly follow'd by the fleeting gloom.
O Night! thy smiles are short, and short thy shade;

Thou art a freakish friend, and all unstay'd:
Yet from thy varied changes who are free?
Full many an honest friend resembles thee.
Then let my doubtful footsteps darkling stray,
Thy next fair beam will set me on my way:
E'en take thy freedom, whether rough or kind,
I came not forth to quarrel with the wind.

TO FEAR.

O thou! before whose haggard eyes
A thousand images arise,
Whose forms of horror none may see,
But with a soul disturb'd by thee!
Wilt thon for ever haunt mankind,
And glare upon the darken'd mind!
Whene'er thou enterest a breast,
Thou robb'st it of its joy and rest;
And terrible, and strange to tell,
On what that mind delights to dwell.
The ruffian's knife with reeking blade,
The stranger murder'd in his bed:
The howling wind, the raging deep,
The sailor's cries, the sinking ship:
The awful thunder breaking round:
The yauning gulf, the rocking ground:
The precipice, whose low'ring brow
O'erhangs the horrid deep below;
And tempts the wretch, worn out with strife,
Of worldly cares, to end his life.

But when thou raisest to the fight
Unearthly forms that walk the night,
The chilly blood, with magic art,
Runs backward on the stoutest heart.
Lo! in his post the soldier stands[See Spectator, No. 12.]!
The deadly weapon in his hands.
In front of death he rushes on,
Renown with life is cheaply won,
Whilst all his soul with ardour burns,
And to the thickest danger turns.
But see the man alone, unbent,
A church-yard near, and twilight spent,
Returning late to his abode,
Upon an unfrequented road:
No choice is left, his feet must tread
The awful dwelling of the dead.
In foul mist doth the pale moon wade,
No twinkling star breaks thro' the shade:
Thick rows of trees increase the gloom,
And awful silence of the tomb.
Swift to his thoughts, unbidden, throng
Full many a tale, forgotten long,
Of ghosts, who at the dead of night
Walk round their graves all wrapt in white,
And o'er the church-yard dark and drear,
Becken the traveller to draw near:
And restless sprites, who from the ground,
Just as the midnight clock doth sound,
Rise slowly to a dreadful height,
Then vanish quickly from the fight:
And wretches who, returning home,
By chance have stumbled near some tomb,
Athwart a coffin or a bone,

And three times heard a hollow groan;
With fearful steps he takes his way,
And shrinks, and wishes it were day.
He starts and quakes at his own tread,
But dare not turn about his head.
Some sound he hears on ev'ry side;
And thro' the trees strange phantoms glide.
His heart beats thick against his breast,
And hardly stays within its chest:
Wild and unsettled are his eyes;
His quicken'd hairs begin to rise:
Ghastly and strong his features grow;
The cold dew trickles from his brow;
Whilst grinning beat his clatt'ring teeth,
And loosen'd knock his joints beneath.
As to the charnel he draws nigh
The whiten'd tomb-stone strikes his eye:
He starts, he stops, his eye-balls glare,
And settle in a death-like stare:
Deep hollow sounds ring in his ear;
Such sounds as dying wretches hear
When the grim dreaded tyrant calls,
A horrid sound, he groans and falls.

  Thou do'st our fairest hope destroy;
Thou art a gloom o'er ev'ry joy;
Unheeded let my dwelling be,
O Fear! but far remov'd from thee!

A STORY OF OTHER TIMES.

SOMEWHAT IN IMITATION OF THE POEMS OF OSSIAN.

LATHMOR.
But why do'st thou stop on the way, and hold me thus hard in thy grasp?
It was but the voice of the winds from the deep narrow glens of Glanarven.

ALLEN.
The heath is unruffled around, and the oak o'er thy head is at rest:
Calm swells the moon on the lake, and nothing is heard in the reeds.
Sad was the sound, O my father! but it was not the voice of the wind.

LATHMOR.
What dark tow'ring rock do I see 'midst the grey spreading mist of the
hills?
This is not the vale of Clanarven: my son, we have err'd from the way,

ALLEN.
It is not a dark tow'ring rock, 'midst the grey settled mist of the hills.
'Tis a dark tow'r of strength which thou seest, and the ocean spreads
dimly behind it.

LATHMOR.
Then here will we stop for the night, for the tow'r of Arthula is near.
Proceed not, my son, on the way, for it was not the voice of the wind.
The ghost of the valliant is forth; and it mourns round the place of its
woe.
The tray'ller oft' hears it at midnight, and turns him aside from its
haunt.
The sharp moon is spent in her course, and the way of the desert is

doubtful.

This oak with his wide leavy branches will shelter our heads from the night;

And I'll tell thee a story of old, since the tow'r of Arthula is near.

From the walls of his strength came Lochallen, with his broad chested sons of the hills.

He was strong as a bull of the forest, and keen as a bird of the rock.

His friends of the chace were around him, the sons of the heroes of Mora.

They were clad in the strength of their youth; and the sound of their arms rung afar.

For Uthal had led his dark host from the blue misty isle of his power;

And o'erspread like a cloud of the desert, the land of the white-headed Lorma.

Of Lorma who sat in the hall, and lamented the sons of his youth;

For Orvina remained alone to support the frail steps of his age.

He sent to the king of Ithona: he remembered the love of his father:

And Lochallen soon join'd him on Loarn with the high minded chieftains of Mora.

Loud was the sound of the battle, and many the slain of the field.

Red was the sword of Lochallen: it was red with the blood of the brave.

For his eye sought the combat of heroes, and the mighty withstood not his arm.

He rag'd like a flame on the heath; and the enemy fled from his face.

But short was the triumph of Lorma; the hour of his fading was near.

Whilst a bard rais'd the song of the battle, his dim eyes were closed in death.

He fell like a ruined tow'r; like a fragment of times that are past:

Like a rock whose foundation is worn with the lashes of many a wave.

Four grey head warriors of Lorma remain'd from the days of his youth:

They mourn'd o'er the fall of their lord; and they bore him to his dark narrow house.

His memorial was rais'd on the hill; and the lovely Orvina wept over it.

She bent her fair form o'er the heap; and her sorrow was silent, and gentle.

It flow'd like the pure twinkling dream beneath the green shade of the fern.

The hunters oft bless it at noon, tho' the strangers perceive not its course.

The wind of the hill rais'd her locks, and Lochallen beheld her in grief.

The soul of the hero was knit to the tear-eyed daughter of Lorma.

She was graceful and tall as the willow, that bends o'er the deep shady stream.

Her eye like a sun-beam on water, that gleams thro' the dark skirting reeds.

Her hair like the light wreathing cloud, that floats on the brow of the hill,

When the beam of the morning is there, and it scatters its skirts to the wind.

Lovely and soft were her smiles, like a glimpse from the white riven cloud,

When the sun hastens over the lake, and a summer show'r ruffles its bosom.

Her voice was the sweet sound of midnight, that visits the ear of the bard,

When he darts from the place of his slumber, and calls on some far distant friend.

She was fair 'mongst the maids of her time; and she soften'd the wrath of the mighty.

Their eyes lighten'd up in her presence; they dropt their dark spears as she spoke.

Lochallen was firm in his strength, and unmov'd in the battle of heroes;

Like a rock-fenced isle of the ocean, that shews its dark head thro' the storm.

His brow was like a cliff on the shore, that fore-warneth the hunters of

Ithona;

For there gleams the first ray of morning, and there broods the mist ere the storm:

It shone, and it darken'd by turns, as the strength of his passions arose.

He was terrible as a gathering storm, when his soul learnt the wrongs of the feeble.

His eye was the lightning of shields; he was swift as a blast in its course.

When the warriors return'd from the field, and the sons of the mighty assembled,

He was graceful as the light tow'ring cloud that rises from the blue bounded main.

Gentle and fair was his form in the tow'rs of the hilly Ithona.

His voice cheer'd the soul of the sad; he would sport with a child in the hall.

Matchless in the days of their love were Lochallen and the daughter of Lorma.

But their beauty has ceas'd on Arthula; and the place of their rest is unknown.

The family of Lorma has fail'd, and strangers rejoice in his hall:

But voices of sorrow are heard when the stillness of midnight is there;

The stranger is wak'd with the sound, and enquires of the race that is gone.

But wherefore thus doleful and sad, do ye wander alone on Arthula?

Why look ye thus lonely and sad, ye children of the dark narrow house?

Your names shall be known in the song, when the fame of the mighty is low.

ALLEN.

From what cloud of the hills do they look? for I see not their forms, O my father!

LATHMOR.

Why do'st thou tremble my son? thou hast fought in the battle of shields.
They look'd from no cloud of the hills; but the soul of thy father beheld
them.
Lochallen return'd from the field, to the sea-beaten tower of Arthula.
Five days he abode in the hall, and they pass'd like a glimpse of the sun,
When the clouds of the tempest are rent, and the green island smiles
'midst the storm.
On the sixth a cloud hung on his brow, and his eye shun'd the looks of his
friends.
He spoke to the maid of his soul, and the trouble of his bosom was great.
Pleasant is the hall of my love; but the storm gathers round us, Orvina.
I must go to the island of Uthal, and scatter his gathering force.
But like a cleft oak of the forest, I'll quickly return to my love:
When the hard wedge is drawn from its side, it returns to itself again.
The daughter of Lorma was silent: she turn'd her fair face from his sight.
Go to the war, son of Mora; and the strength of thy fathers go with thee.
I will sit on the high rocky shore, and look o'er the wide foaming sea.
I will watch ev'ry blue rising cloud, till I see thy dark vessels return.

He gather'd his warriours around him; they darken'd the brown rugged
shore.
The rocks echo'd wide to their cries, and loud was the dashing of oars.
Orvina stood high on a rock, that hung o'er the deep lashing main;
Big swell'd the tear in her eye, and high heav'd the sighs of her bosom;
As she saw the white billows encreasing between his dark ship and the
shore.
Her fixed eye follow'd its course o'er many a far distant wave,
Till its broad sails, and high tow'ring mast but appear'd like a speck on
the waters;
Yet still she beheld in her fancy the form of her love on its side;
And she stretched her white arms to the ocean, and wav'd her loose girdle
on high.

Soon reach'd the sons of Ithona the blue misty isle of their foe.

Like the pent up dogs of the hunter when let loose from their prison of night;

Who snuff up the air of the morning, and rejoice at the voice of the chace;

They leapt from the sides of their vessels, and spread o'er the wide sounding shore.

Thick on the brown heathy plain, were spread the dark thousands of Uthal.

The warriours of Lochallen were few, but their fathers were known in the song.

Like a small rapid stream of the hills when it falls on the broad settled lake,

And troubles its dark muddy bosom, and dashes its waters aloft,

So rush'd the keen sons of Ithona on the thick gather'd host of the foe.

Red gleam'd the arms of the brave thro' the brown rising dust of the field.

Fierce glar'd the eyes of Lochallen; he fought the dark face of his enemy.

He found the grim king of the isle; but the strength of his chieftains was round him.

Come forth in thy might, said Lochallen; come forth to the combat of kings.

Great is the might of thy warriours; but where is the strength of thine arms?

Youth of Ithona, said Uthal, thy fathers were mighty in battle,

Return to thy brown woody hills, till the hair is grown dark on thy cheek;

Then come from the tow'rs of thy safety, a foe less unworthy of Uthal.

But thou lovest a weakly enemy, foe of the white haired chief.

Thou lovest a foe that is weak, said the red swelling pride of Lochallen.

Seest thou this sword of my youth? it is red with the blood of thy heroes.

Come forth in the strength of thine years, and hand its dark blade in thy hall.

He lifted a spear in his wrath o'er the head of his high worded foe;

But the strength of his chieftains was there, and it rung on their broad spreading shields.

He turned himself scornful away, to look for some nobler enemy;

He met thee fair son of Hidallo, as chaffing he strode in his wrath;

But thou never did'st turn from the valiant, youth of the far distant
land.

Fierce fought the heroes, and wonder'd each chief at the might of his foe.

They found themselves matched in strength, and they fought in the pride of
their souls.

Bloody and long was the fight, but the arm of Lochallen prevail'd.

Ah, why did you combat, ye heroes! ah, why did ye meet in the field!

Your souls had been brothers of love, had ye met in the dwellings of
peace.

He was like to thyself, son of Mora, where his voice cheer'd the heart of
the stranger

In the far distant hall of his father, who never shall hear it again;

He was like to thyself whom thou slewest; and he fell in his youth like
thee.

The maid of thy bosom is lovely, thou fair fallen son of the stranger.

She sits on her high hanging bower, and looks to the way of thy promise.

She combs down her long yellow hair; and prepares a fine robe for thy
coming.

She starts at the voice of the breeze, and runs to the door of her bow'r.

But thou art a dim misty form on the clouds of far distant hills.

Fierce was the rage of the battle, and terrible the clanging of arms.

Loud were the shouts of the mighty, like the wide scatter'd thunder of
Lora,

When its voice is return'd from the rocks, and it strengthens in its broad
spreading course.

Heavy were the groans of the dying; the voice of the fallen was sad,

Like the deep 'prison'd winds of the cavern, when the roar of the tempest
is laid.

The sons of Ithona were terrible: the enemy fled from before them,

Like the dark gather'd fowls of the ocean, that flock to the shore ere a
storm.
They fled from the might of their foes, and the darkness of night clos'd
around them.

Cold rose the wind of the desert, and blew o'er the dark bloody field.
Sad was its voice on the heath, where it lifted the locks of the dead.
Hollow roar'd the sea at a distance: the ghosts of the slain shriek'd
aloud.
Pale shady forms stalk'd around, and their airy swords gleam'd thro' the
night;
For the spirits of warriours departed came born on the deep rushing blast;
There hail'd they their new fallen sons, and the sound of their meeting
was terrible.
At a distance was gather'd Ithona round many a bright flaming oak;
Till morning rose red o'er the main, like a new bloody field of battle.

Lochallen assembled his heroes; they rang'd o'er the land of their enemy.
But they found not the king in the field; and the walls of his strength
were deserted.
Then spoke the friend of his bosom, the dark haired chief of Trevallen;
Why seek you the king in his tow'rs? he is fled to the caves of his fear.
Let us fly, said the chief of Ithona, let us fly to the daughter of Lorma!
Let us fight with man in the field, but pull not a deer from his den.

Two days they buried their dead, and rais'd their memorial on high.
On the third day they loosen'd their vessels, and left the blue isle of
their fame.
The darkness of night was around when the bay of Arthula receiv'd them.
Thick beat the joy of his bosom, as he drew near the place of his love;
But the strength of his limbs was unloos'd, as he trode on the dark
sounding shore.
Thou did'st promise, O maid of my soul! thou did'st promise to watch for

thy love!

But no kindly messenger waits to hail my return from the war.

The tow'r of Arthula is dark; and I hear not the sound of its hall.

The watch dog howls to the night, nor heeds the approach of our feet.

He seized a bright flaming brand, and he hasten'd his steps to the tow'r.

Wide stood the black low'ring gate; and deep was the silence within.

Hollow and loud rung his steps, as he trode thro' the dark empty hall.

He flew to the bow'r of his love; it was still as the chamber of death.

His eyes search'd wildly around him; he call'd on the name of his love;

But his own voice returned alone from the deep-sounding walls of the tow'r.

He leant with his back to the wall, and cross'd his arms over his breast.

Heavy sunk his head on his shoulder: the blue flame burnt double before him.

A voice, like the evening breeze when it steals down the bed of the river,

Came softly and sad to his ear, and he raised his drooping head.

The form of his love stood before him: yet it was not the form of his love;

For fixed and dim was her eye, and the beams of her beauty were fled.

She was pale as the white frozen lake, when it gleams to the light of the moon.

Her garments were heavy and drench'd, and the streams trickled fast from her hair.

She was like a snow-crusted tree in winter, when it drops to the mid-day sun.

O seek not for me, son of Moro, in the light cheerful dwellings of men!

For low is my bed in the deep, and cold is the place of my rest.

The sea monster sports by my side, and the water-snake twines round my neck.

But do not forget me, Lochallen: O think on the days of our love!

I sat on the high rocky shore, mine eyes look'd afar o'er the ocean.

I saw two dark ships on the waves, and quick beat the joy of my breast.

One vessel drew near to the shore, and six warriors leapt from its side.

I hasten'd to meet thee, my love; but mine ear met the stern voice of
Uthal.
I thought that my hero was slain, and I felt me alone in my weakness.
I felt me deserted and lonely: I flew to the steep hanging rock:
I threw my robe over my head; and I hid me in the dark closing deep.
Yet O do not leave me, Lochallen, to waste in my watery bed!
But raise me a tomb on the hill, where the daughter of Lorma should lie.
The voice of her sorrow did cease; and her form passed quickly away.
It pass'd like the pale shiv'ring light, that is lost in the dark closing
cloud.

But, lo! the first light of the morning is red on the skirts of the
heavens.
Let us go on my journey, my son, for the length of the heath is before us.

ALLEN.
It is not the light of the morn which thou see'st on the skirts of the
heavens;
It is but a clear shiv'ring brightness, that changes its hue to the night.
I have seen it like a bloody-spread robe when it hung o'er the waves of
the North.
Sad was the fate of his love, but how fell the king of Ithona?
I have heard of the strength of his arm; did he fall in the battle of
heroes?

LATHMOR.
He fell in the strength of his youth, but he fell not in battle, my son.
He knew not the sword of a foe, yet he died not the death of the peaceful.
They carried them both to the hill, but the place of their rest is
unknown.

ALLEN.
But feeble and spent is thy voice, thou grey haired bard of the hill.

LATHMOR.
Long is this song of the night, and I feel not the strength of my youth.

ALLEN.
Then let us go on our way: let us go by the way of the heath.
For it is the fair light of the morning which thou see'st on the far bounding waves.
Slowly it grows in its beauty, and promises good to the traveller.
Red are the small broken clouds that hang on the skirts of the heavens.
Deep glows the clear open sky with the light of the yet hidden sun,
Save where the dark narrow cloud hath stretched its vast length o'er the heavens;
And the clear ruddy brightness behind it looks fair thro' its blue streaming lines.
A bloom like the far distant heath is dark on the wide roving clouds.
The broad wavy breast of the ocean is grand in the beauty of morning.
Thick rests the white settled mist on the deep rugged clifts of the shore;
And the grey rocks look dimly between, like the high distant isles in a calm.
But grim low'r the walks of Arthula; the light of the morn is behind them.

LATHMOR.
Dark low'rs the tow'r of Arthula: the time of its glory is past.
The valiant have ceas'd from its hall; and the son of the stranger is there.
The works of the mighty remain, but they are the vapour of morning.

A MOTHER TO HER WAKING INFANT.

Now in thy dazzling half-op'd eye,
Thy curled nose, and lip awry,
Thy up-hoist arms, and noddling head,
And little chin with crystal spread,
Poor helpless thing! what do I see,
  That I should sing of thee?

From thy poor tongue no accents come,
Which can but rub thy toothless gum:
Small understanding boast thy face,
Thy shapeless limbs nor step, nor grace:
A few short words thy feats may tell,
  And yet I love thee well.

When sudden wakes the bitter shriek,
And redder swells thy little cheek;
When rattled keys thy woe beguile,
And thro' the wet eye gleams the smile,
Still for thy weakly self is spent
  Thy little silly plaint.

But when thy friends are in distress,
Thou'lt laugh and chuckle ne'er the less;
Nor e'en with sympathy be smitten,
Tho' all are sad but thee and kitten;
Yet little varlet that thou art,
  Thou twitchest at the heart.

Thy rosy cheek so soft and warm;

Thy pinky hand, and dimpled arm;
Thy silken locks that scantly peep,
With gold-tip'd ends, where circle deep
Around thy neck in harmless grace
So soft and sleekly hold their place,
Might harder hearts with kindness fill,
  And gain our right good will.

Each passing clown bestows his blessing,
Thy mouth is worn with old wives' kissing:
E'en lighter looks the gloomy eye
Of surly sense, when thou art by;
And yet I think whoe'er they be,
  They love thee not like me.

Perhaps when time shall add a few
Short years to thee, thou'lt love me too.
Then wilt thou thro' life's weary way
Become my sure and cheering stay:
Wilt care, for me, and be my hold,
  When I am weak and old.

Thou'lt listen to my lengthen'd tale,
And pity me when I am frail--
But see, the sweepy spinning fly
Upon the window takes thine eye.
Go to thy little senseless play--
  Thou doest not heed my lay.

A CHILD TO HIS SICK GRANDFATHER.

Grand-dad, they say your old and frail,
Your stocked legs begin to fail:
Your knobbed stick (that was my horse)
Can scarce support your bended corse;
While back to wall, you lean so sad,
  I'm vex'd to see you, dad.

You us'd to smile, and stroke my head,
And tell me how good children did;
But now I wot not how it be,
You take me seldom on your knee;
Yet ne'ertheless I am right glad
  To sit beside you, dad.

How lank and thin your beard hangs down!
Scant are the white hairs on your crown:
How wan and hollow are your cheeks!
Your brow is rough with crossing breaks;
But yet, for all his strength is fled,
  I love my own old dad.

The housewives round their potions brew,
And gossips come to ask for you:
And for your weal each neighbour cares,
And good men kneel, and say their pray'rs:
And ev'ry body looks so sad,
  When you are ailing, dad.

You will not die, and leave us then?

Rouse up and be our dad again.
When you are quiet and laid in bed,
We'll doff our shoes and softly tread;
And when you wake we'll aye be near,
  To fill old dad his cheer.

When thro' the house you shift your stand,
I'll lead you kindly by the hand:
When dinner's set, I'll with you bide,
And aye be serving by your side:
And when the weary fire burns blue,
  I'll sit and talk with you.

I have a tale both long and good,
About a partlet and her brood;
And cunning greedy fox, that stole,
By dead of midnight thro' a hole,
Which slyly to the hen-roost led--
  You love a story, dad?

And then I have a wond'rous tale
Of men all clad in coats of mail.
With glitt'ring swords----you nod, I think?
Your fixed eyes begin to wink:
Down on your bosom sinks your head:
You do not hear me, dad.

THE HORSE AND HIS RIDER.

Brac'd in the sinewy vigour of thy breed,
In pride of gen'rous strength, thou stately steed,

Thy broad chest to the battle's front is given,
Thy mane fair floating to the winds of heaven.
Thy champing hoofs the flinty pebbles break;
Graceful the rising of thine arched neck.
White churning foam thy chaffed bits enlock;
And from thy nostril bursts the curling smoke.
Thy kindling eye-balls brave the glaring south;
And dreadful is the thunder of thy mouth:
Whilst low to earth thy curving haunches bend,
Thy sweepy tail involv'd in clouds of sand;
Erect in air thou rear'st thy front of pride,
And ring'st the plated harness on thy side.
But, lo! what creature, goodly to the sight,
Dares thus bestride thee, chaffing in thy might?
Of portly stature, and determin'd mien?
Whose dark eye dwells beneath a brow serene?
And forward looks unmov'd to fields of death:
And smiling, gently strokes thee in thy wrath?
Whose brandish'd falch'on dreaded gleams afar?
It is a British soldier, arm'd for war!

FINIS.

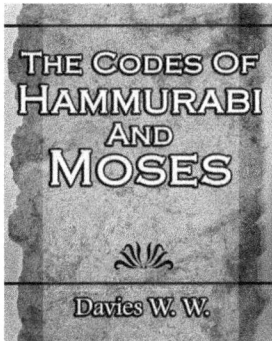

The Codes Of Hammurabi And Moses
W. W. Davies

QTY

The discovery of the Hammurabi Code is one of the greatest achievements of archaeology, and is of paramount interest, not only to the student of the Bible, but also to all those interested in ancient history...

Religion   **ISBN:** *1-59462-338-4*   **Pages:132**
MSRP $12.95

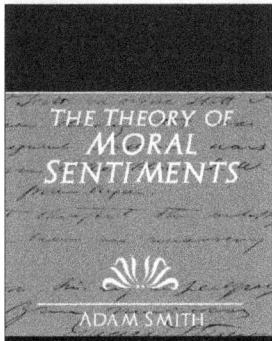

The Theory of Moral Sentiments
Adam Smith

QTY

This work from 1749. contains original theories of conscience amd moral judgment and it is the foundation for systemof morals.

Philosophy **ISBN:** *1-59462-777-0*   **Pages:536**
MSRP $19.95

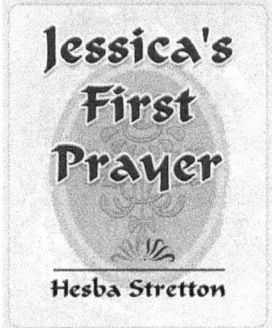

Jessica's First Prayer
Hesba Stretton

QTY

In a screened and secluded corner of one of the many railway-bridges which span the streets of London there could be seen a few years ago, from five o'clock every morning until half past eight, a tidily set-out coffee-stall, consisting of a trestle and board, upon which stood two large tin cans, with a small fire of charcoal burning under each so as to keep the coffee boiling during the early hours of the morning when the work-people were thronging into the city on their way to their daily toil...

Childrens   **ISBN:** *1-59462-373-2*   **Pages:84**
MSRP $9.95

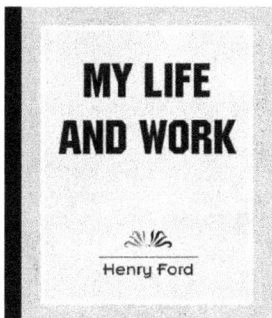

My Life and Work
Henry Ford

QTY

Henry Ford revolutionized the world with his implementation of mass production for the Model T automobile. Gain valuable business insight into his life and work with his own auto-biography... "We have only started on our development of our country we have not as yet, with all our talk of wonderful progress, done more than scratch the surface. The progress has been wonderful enough but..."

Biographies/   **ISBN:** *1-59462-198-5*   **Pages:300**
MSRP $21.95

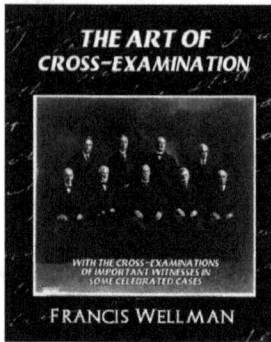

The Art of Cross-Examination
Francis Wellman

QTY

I presume it is the experience of every author, after his first book is published upon an important subject, to be almost overwhelmed with a wealth of ideas and illustrations which could readily have been included in his book, and which to his own mind, at least, seem to make a second edition inevitable. Such certainly was the case with me; and when the first edition had reached its sixth impression in five months, I rejoiced to learn that it seemed to my publishers that the book had met with a sufficiently favorable reception to justify a second and considerably enlarged edition. ..

Reference   ISBN: *1-59462-647-2*

Pages:412

MSRP $19.95

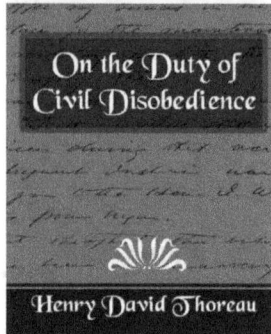

On the Duty of Civil Disobedience
Henry David Thoreau

QTY

Thoreau wrote his famous essay, On the Duty of Civil Disobedience, as a protest against an unjust but popular war and the immoral but popular institution of slave-owning. He did more than write—he declined to pay his taxes, and was hauled off to gaol in consequence. Who can say how much this refusal of his hastened the end of the war and of slavery ?

Law   ISBN: *1-59462-747-9*

Pages:48

MSRP $7.45

Dream Psychology Psychoanalysis for Beginners
Sigmund Freud

QTY

Sigmund Freud, born Sigismund Schlomo Freud (May 6, 1856 - September 23, 1939), was a Jewish-Austrian neurologist and psychiatrist who co-founded the psychoanalytic school of psychology. Freud is best known for his theories of the unconscious mind, especially involving the mechanism of repression; his redefinition of sexual desire as mobile and directed towards a wide variety of objects; and his therapeutic techniques, especially his understanding of transference in the therapeutic relationship and the presumed value of dreams as sources of insight into unconscious desires.

Psychology   ISBN: *1-59462-905-6*

Pages:196

MSRP $15.45

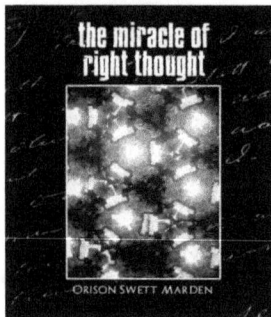

The Miracle of Right Thought
Orison Swett Marden

QTY

Believe with all of your heart that you will do what you were made to do. When the mind has once formed the habit of holding cheerful, happy, prosperous pictures, it will not be easy to form the opposite habit. It does not matter how improbable or how far away this realization may see, or how dark the prospects may be, if we visualize them as best we can, as vividly as possible, hold tenaciously to them and vigorously struggle to attain them, they will gradually become actualized, realized in the life. But a desire, a longing without endeavor, a yearning abandoned or held indifferently will vanish without realization.

Pages:360

Self Help   ISBN: *1-59462-644-8*

MSRP $25.45

QTY

☐ **The Rosicrucian Cosmo-Conception Mystic Christianity** *by Max Heindel*   ISBN: *1-59462-188-8* **$38.95**
The Rosicrucian Cosmo-conception is not dogmatic, neither does it appeal to any other authority than the reason of the student. It is: not controversial, but is: sent forth in the, hope that it may help to clear...   New Age/Religion Pages 646

☐ **Abandonment To Divine Providence** *by Jean-Pierre de Caussade*   ISBN: *1-59462-228-0* **$25.95**
"The Rev. Jean Pierre de Caussade was one of the most remarkable spiritual writers of the Society of Jesus in France in the 18th Century. His death took place at Toulouse in 1751. His works have gone through many editions and have been republished...   Inspirational/Religion Pages 400

☐ **Mental Chemistry** *by Charles Haanel*   ISBN: *1-59462-192-6* **$23.95**
Mental Chemistry allows the change of material conditions by combining and appropriately utilizing the power of the mind. Much like applied chemistry creates something new and unique out of careful combinations of chemicals the mastery of mental chemistry...   New Age Pages 354

☐ **The Letters of Robert Browning and Elizabeth Barret Barrett 1845-1846 vol II**   ISBN: *1-59462-193-4* **$35.95**
by Robert Browning and Elizabeth Barrett   Biographies Pages 596

☐ **Gleanings In Genesis (volume I)** *by Arthur W. Pink*   ISBN: *1-59462-130-6* **$27.45**
Appropriately has Genesis been termed "the seed plot of the Bible" for in it we have, in germ form, almost all of the great doctrines which are afterwards fully developed in the books of Scripture which follow...   Religion/Inspirational Pages 420

☐ **The Master Key** *by L. W. de Laurence*   ISBN: *1-59462-001-6* **$30.95**
In no branch of human knowledge has there been a more lively increase of the spirit of research during the past few years than in the study of Psychology, Concentration and Mental Discipline. The requests for authentic lessons in Thought Control, Mental Discipline and...   New Age/Business Pages 422

☐ **The Lesser Key Of Solomon Goetia** *by L. W. de Laurence*   ISBN: *1-59462-092-X* **$9.95**
This translation of the first book of the "Lemegton" which is now for the first time made accessible to students of Talismanic Magic was done, after careful collation and edition, from numerous Ancient Manuscripts in Hebrew, Latin, and French...   New Age/Occult Pages 92

☐ **Rubaiyat Of Omar Khayyam** *by Edward Fitzgerald*   ISBN:*1-59462-332-5* **$13.95**
Edward Fitzgerald, whom the world has already learned, in spite of his own efforts to remain within the shadow of anonymity, to look upon as one of the rarest poets of the century, was born at Bredfield, in Suffolk, on the 31st of March, 1809. He was the third son of John Purcell...   Music Pages 172

☐ **Ancient Law** *by Henry Maine*   ISBN: *1-59462-128-4* **$29.95**
The chief object of the following pages is to indicate some of the earliest ideas of mankind, as they are reflected in Ancient Law, and to point out the relation of those ideas to modern thought.   Religiom/History Pages 452

☐ **Far-Away Stories** *by William J. Locke*   ISBN: *1-59462-129-2* **$19.45**
"Good wine needs no bush, but a collection of mixed vintages does. And this book is just such a collection. Some of the stories I do not want to remain buried for ever in the museum files of dead magazine-numbers an author's not unpardonable vanity..."   Fiction Pages 272

☐ **Life of David Crockett** *by David Crockett*   ISBN: *1-59462-250-7* **$27.45**
"Colonel David Crockett was one of the most remarkable men of the times in which he lived. Born in humble life, but gifted with a strong will, an indomitable courage, and unremitting perseverance...   Biographies/New Age Pages 424

☐ **Lip-Reading** *by Edward Nitchie*   ISBN: *1-59462-206-X* **$25.95**
Edward B. Nitchie, founder of the New York School for the Hard of Hearing, now the Nitchie School of Lip-Reading, Inc, wrote "LIP-READING Principles and Practice". The development and perfecting of this meritorious work on lip-reading was an undertaking...   How-to Pages 400

☐ **A Handbook of Suggestive Therapeutics, Applied Hypnotism, Psychic Science**   ISBN: *1-59462-214-0* **$24.95**
by Henry Munro   Health/New Age/Health/Self-help Pages 376

☐ **A Doll's House: and Two Other Plays** *by Henrik Ibsen*   ISBN: *1-59462-112-8* **$19.95**
Henrik Ibsen created this classic when in revolutionary 1848 Rome. Introducing some striking concepts in playwriting for the realist genre, this play has been studied the world over.   Fiction/Classics/Plays 308

☐ **The Light of Asia** *by sir Edwin Arnold*   ISBN: *1-59462-204-3* **$13.95**
In this poetic masterpiece, Edwin Arnold describes the life and teachings of Buddha. The man who was to become known as Buddha to the world was born as Prince Gautama of India but he rejected the worldly riches and abandoned the reigns of power when...   Religion/History/Biographies Pages 170

☐ **The Complete Works of Guy de Maupassant** *by Guy de Maupassant*   ISBN: *1-59462-157-8* **$16.95**
"For days and days, nights and nights, I had dreamed of that first kiss which was to consecrate our engagement, and I knew not on what spot I should put my lips..."   Fiction/Classics Pages 240

☐ **The Art of Cross-Examination** *by Francis L. Wellman*   ISBN: *1-59462-309-0* **$26.95**
Written by a renowned trial lawyer, Wellman imparts his experience and uses case studies to explain how to use psychology to extract desired information through questioning.   How-to/Science/Reference Pages 408

☐ **Answered or Unanswered?** *by Louisa Vaughan*   ISBN: *1-59462-248-5* **$10.95**
Miracles of Faith in China   Religion Pages 112

☐ **The Edinburgh Lectures on Mental Science (1909)** *by Thomas*   ISBN: *1-59462-008-3* **$11.95**
This book contains the substance of a course of lectures recently given by the writer in the Queen Street Hail, Edinburgh. Its purpose is to indicate the Natural Principles governing the relation between Mental Action and Material Conditions...   New Age/Psychology Pages 148

☐ **Ayesha** *by H. Rider Haggard*   ISBN: *1-59462-301-5* **$24.95**
Verily and indeed it is the unexpected that happens! Probably if there was one person upon the earth from whom the Editor of this, and of a certain previous history, did not expect to hear again...   Classics Pages 380

☐ **Ayala's Angel** *by Anthony Trollope*   ISBN: *1-59462-352-X* **$29.95**
The two girls were both pretty, but Lucy who was twenty-one who supposed to be simple and comparatively unattractive, whereas Ayala was credited, as her Bombwhat romantic name might show, with poetic charm and a taste for romance. Ayala when her father died was nineteen...   Fiction Pages 484

☐ **The American Commonwealth** *by James Bryce*   ISBN: *1-59462-286-8* **$34.45**
An interpretation of American democratic political theory. It examines political mechanics and society from the perspective of Scotsman James Bryce   Politics Pages 572

☐ **Stories of the Pilgrims** *by Margaret P. Pumphrey*   ISBN: *1-59462-116-0* **$17.95**
This book explores pilgrims religious oppression in England as well as their escape to Holland and eventual crossing to America on the Mayflower, and their early days in New England...   History Pages 268

QTY

The Fasting Cure *by Sinclair Upton*   ISBN: *1-59462-222-1* **$13.95**
In the Cosmopolitan Magazine for May, 1910, and in the Contemporary Review (London) for April, 1910, I published an article dealing with my experi-
ences in fasting. I have written a great many magazine articles, but never one which attracted so much attention... New Age/Self Help/Health Pages 164

Hebrew Astrology *by Sepharial*   ISBN: *1-59462-308-2* **$13.45**
In these days of advanced thinking it is a matter of common observation that we have left many of the old landmarks behind and that we are now pressing
forward to greater heights and to a wider horizon than that which represented the mind-content of our progenitors...   Astrology Pages 144

Thought Vibration or The Law of Attraction in the Thought World   ISBN: *1-59462-127-6* **$12.95**
by William Walker Atkinson   *Psychology/Religion Pages 144*

Optimism *by Helen Keller*   ISBN: *1-59462-108-X* **$15.95**
Helen Keller was blind, deaf, and mute since 19 months old, yet famously learned how to overcome these handicaps, communicate with the world, and
spread her lectures promoting optimism. An inspiring read for everyone...   Biographies/Inspirational Pages 84

Sara Crewe *by Frances Burnett*   ISBN: *1-59462-360-0*   **$9.45**
In the first place, Miss Minchin lived in London. Her home was a large, dull, tall one, in a large, dull square, where all the houses were alike, and all the
sparrows were alike, and where all the door-knockers made the same heavy sound...   Childrens/Classic Pages 88

The Autobiography of Benjamin Franklin *by Benjamin Franklin*   ISBN: *1-59462-135-7* **$24.95**
The Autobiography of Benjamin Franklin has probably been more extensively read than any other American historical work, and no other book of its kind
has had such ups and downs of fortune. Franklin lived for many years in England, where he was agent...   Biographies/History Pages 332

Name	
Email	
Telephone	
Address	
City, State ZIP	

☐ **Credit Card**   ☐ **Check / Money Order**

Credit Card Number	
Expiration Date	
Signature	

Please Mail to: Book Jungle
                    PO Box 2226
                    Champaign, IL 61825
or Fax to: *630-214-0564*

ORDERING INFORMATION

web: *www.bookjungle.com*
email: *sales@bookjungle.com*
fax: *630-214-0564*
mail: *Book Jungle PO Box 2226 Champaign, IL 61825*
or PayPal *to sales@bookjungle.com*

Please contact us for bulk discounts

DIRECT-ORDER TERMS

**20% Discount if You Order
Two or More Books**
Free Domestic Shipping!
Accepted: Master Card, Visa,
Discover, American Express

www.ingramcontent.com/pod-product-compliance
Lightning Source LLC
Chambersburg PA
CBHW081235090426
42738CB00016B/3310